A Citizen's Guide to the Constitution of the State of Alaska

GORDON S. HARRISON

Foreword by George D. Braden

For Reference

Not to be taken from this room

Institute of Social and Economic Research

University of Alaska

Gordon S. Harrison, Ph.D., formerly an associate professor of political science at the University of Alaska, is now a social science and public affairs consultant in Juneau.

ISBN No. 0-88353-033-3
ISER Report Series Number: 55

Published by:
Institute of Social and Economic Research
University of Alaska
Lee Gorsuch, Director
707 "A" Street, Suite 206
Anchorage, Alaska 99501
1982

Printed in U.S.A.

Foreword

The idea for a citizens' guide to a constitution was John Bebout's. Those of us who are "experts" on state constitutions affectionately call John "Mr. State Constitution." He has worked, advised, and consulted on more state constitutions than anybody else in the history of the United States. He was a consultant to the Alaska Constitutional Convention, naturally. But his influence was greater than his advice to the convention. For example, Dr. Harrison notes on page 40 that Section 16 of Article III is found elsewhere only in New Jersey and the National Municipal League's Model State Constitution. The idea was John's when he was working with the New Jersey Constitutional Convention in 1974.

When John asked me to write the Citizen's Guide to the Texas Constitution (the only other such guide ever written), I took one look at that constitution and saw at once why a guide was needed. The Texas Constitution is one of the longest in the country; it is badly organized, badly written, loaded down with unnecessary detail, and filled with many of the kinds of restrictions that make for weak state government. As I said in the concluding paragraph of the Guide:

> ". . . , the Texas Constitution is cluttered with masses of statutory detail. More important, detail has become the way of life. This bodes ill for the future. If constitutional revision's time has come—the *need* has been evident for decades—will it be possible to make a clean break with this tradition of severe restrictive provisions and great detail? It will not be easy. But if the United States can put men on the moon, surely the people of Texas can draft for themselves a Constitution good for the rest of this century and well into the next."

What I did not say directly in that paragraph was: "Citizens of Texas, you have a lousy constitution. You now have an opportunity to get a new one. Take the opportunity." (Postscript: Texans took the opportunity, were offered a well-organized, well-drafted, modern constitution and turned it down. But that is another story, too sad to tell here.)

The reader of this guide who is knowledgeable about the Alaska Constitution may well ask why Alaskans need a guide. After all, the language of the constitution is relatively simple and concise; it is well organized and is almost wholly free of legislative detail. A general answer is that every state ought to have a guide, partly to explain the constitution to the busy citizen and partly to enlighten all laymen on the basic principles of American constitutions. The specific answer is that the voters of Alaska will be asked at the November 1982 election whether a constitutional convention should be held. In the months before the election, voters who are not knowledgeable about the constitution ought to become familiar with the principles of constitutional government and how their constitution measures up to these principles. The voter who does this can make an informed choice when voting upon the question.

The written constitution, creating a limited government and providing for enforcement of the limitations by an independent agency, the judiciary, is an American invention that the world would do well to adopt. The key elements are "limited government" and "enforcement of the limitations by the judiciary." Ideally, a constitution does only three things: it creates the mechanics of government, what the by-laws of a club do; it sets down the limits on what the government may do and how it may do what is permitted—the bill of Rights, in short; and where there is more than one level of government—nation and states or state and local governments—a constitution distributes power between the two.

An American constitution is the basic document for a *self-governing* people. Ideally, therefore, a constitution ought not deal directly with the problems of government. This is the job of those chosen by the people to govern them. A constitution should be a document for all seasons. It should not try to solve problems; it should state *who* is to solve problems—today's, tomorrow's, and the day after tomorrow's.

Why, one may ask, are the key elements "limited government" and "enforcement by the judiciary?" The purpose of limitations on the government is to protect a minority from the majority of the moment. Obviously, the majority on any single issue is opposed by a minority, but so long as the constitution protects the minority from being destroyed or silenced, the majority remains a majority of the moment. If the reader examines the Bill of Rights in Article I, this purpose of the limitations comes through clearly. Enforcement by the judiciary is necessary because that is the only means by which the instruments of the majority of the moment, the legislative and executive branches, can be restrained.

For many years I was a "pure" purist. I thought that the Bill of Rights should be the only limitation on the power of the majority of the day to decide what the government should do. I changed my view in 1967 when I was working at the New York Constitutional Convention. New York has what is known as the "forever wild" provision. It prevents the alienation of the Adirondack forest preserve except by constitutional amendment. I realized that the majority of the moment could easily destroy an irreplaceable asset of value to the majorities of the future. Thus, I commend the Alaska Constitutional Convention for its Natural Resources Article VIII and the voters of Alaska on the subsequent addition of Section 15 of Article IX creating the Alaska Permanent Fund. These are two instances of the recognition by a society that the desires of the present generation should be subordinated to the long-range interests of future generations.

As one reads the Alaska Constitution, one will find that it follows these principles of the ideal constitution. But the constitution does more. It avoids the errors of many state constitutions. It avoids what I call "special" limitations as opposed to the "general" limitations that are represented by a Bill of Rights and provisions designed to protect future majorities from the short-range interests of today's majorities. Examples of special limitations are endless. A few constitutional examples: a prohibition on gambling; a prohibition on an income tax; a limitation on the amount of money that can be raised by property taxes; a prohibition against gifts or loans to private individuals or corporations. In essence, these special limitations are protections of the majority against themselves. It is a confession of the voters' inability to elect representatives who will do what the majority want. Many state constitutions contain special limitations of this sort. Alaskans may not be aware of this constitutional fault because the Alaska Constitution has almost none of them. Thus, another plus for the Alaska Constitution; the evils of bad constitutions were avoided.

In the Texas Guide I had this to say about the section that granted home rule to cities: "In this sometimes lugubrious tour through the Constitution, it is pleasant to point out that Section 5 as interpreted is a relatively rare gem in state constituions." What made it a gem was that the Texas Supreme Court said that Section 5 permits a home-rule city to exercise any legislative power that the legislature does not deny to the cities. This is what Section 11 of Article X specifically provides. Here again the Alaska Constitutional Convention opted for the best that students of state constitutions recommend. I must note, however, that the Alaska Supreme Court has handed down some opinions that narrow this broad grant of home-rule power. (See Sharp, "Home Rule in Alaska" *UCLA-Alaska Law*

Review [Fall, 1973]: 1-54.) This is simply one of the costs of permitting the judiciary to interpret the constitution. If we are to depend upon the courts to keep the legislative and executive branches within the limits we set for government, we must be prepared to accept judicial errors. You can't win 'em all.

I do not say that the Alaska Constitution is perfect. As Dr. Harrison points out, most of the substantive provisions of Article VI, Legislative Apportionment, are nullities because of the United States Supreme Court's "one person-one vote" requirement under the Equal Protection Clause of the Fourteenth Amendment. But imperfection is not a criterion for determining whether a constitutional convention is needed. Amendment on the initiative of the legislature is available to remove imperfections and has been used a number of times in Alaska, generally to good purpose. The criterion for holding a convention is a determination by the voters that they are not happy with their basic document as a whole and want an independent review of it.

To protect this power of the people, many state constitutions require a periodic submission to the voters of this question of an independent review, for legislatures cannot be depended upon to initiate a convention that might encroach on their turf. The period traditionally has been 20 years, a magic number derived from Thomas Jefferson. The delegates to the Alaska Convention recognized this need for going directly to the people, but in the spirit of rapid change they cut the time in half. We "experts" think this was a mistake, but the mistake is not relevant in 1982, for the question is whether a quarter of a century later, the time has come for a comprehensive review of what the 1955-56 Convention wrought—"as amended," of course.

Thus, a generation-plus later, Alaskans have the duty to consider carefully whether the time has come for a comprehensive review of the first convention's product. I would hope only that Alaskans limit that consideration to the constitution as the frame for self-government and not toy with the idea that a constitutional convention would give them the opportunity to "legislate" things that their legislators have failed to do. In a sense, a constitutional convention is a Pandora's Box. The convention has all powers of government and can do anything subject only to the constraints of the United States Constitution and the necessity of subsequent voter approval of their final product. Once a convention convenes, the box is open and anything can happen.

I must confess that personally I do not see the need for a constitutional convention because, as I have made clear, I think Alaska has one of the best of the state constitutions. But I concede that a convention consisting of delegates who would stick to a review of the constitution as a constitution and not wander off the reservation, could serve not only as a useful affirmation of the essential soundness of the original constitution but could recommend such changes as would make a good constitution even better.

In sum, Alaskans have three options, as they say these days. If you like what you have in your constitution and are not sure that a constitutional convention would improve on what you have, the option is to say "no." If you do not like what you have, you obviously say "yes." If you like what you have but would like to improve the constitution and are confident that you can choose delegates who will improve it, the option is to say "yes."

This last option is the best, but only if the delegates by and large are as enlightened as were the Alaskan "founding fathers"—I should say "fathers and mothers." Since they were creating a government from scratch, they approached their task in the spirit of the 55 founding fathers of 1787. Today is different. Alaska has a constitution, an operating government, and the problems of the day. It is easy to focus on these problems and the perceived inadequacy of the operating government and to decide that a constitutional convention can solve everything. This is the road to constitutional disaster. Constitution making is a political process, to be sure. But constitution making is more than that. It is a historical process. That is, today's founding fathers and mothers should deal with the political conflicts of the day in the light of the past and with an eye to the future. Sound constitution making is long range. Most important of all, constitution making is a principle process. Given the politics of the day, given the historical perspective, what should go into a constitution remains a matter of principle—principles of limitations on power, of the mechanics of government, of the distribution of power.

In weighing the pros and cons of a constitutional convention, remember that it is the *system* of government, not the *substance* of government, that is at stake. If a convention is to be held, be sure to elect delegates who understand the principles of constitution making. This will avoid turning the convention into a legislature trying to solve today's problems. This will assure Alaska that its constitution remains what it is today: a document for all seasons.

George D. Braden*

*George D. Braden is an authority on state constitutions and constitutional law. For several years he taught constitutional law at Yale Law School. He is the author of numerous scholarly works on constitutional issues. Among his publications is *Citizen's Guide to The Texas Constitution*.

Acknowledgments

Many people have contributed to this publication by way of comments on the draft manuscript and advice to me as I wrote it. Special thanks are due Richard A. Bradley, George D. Braden, John E. Bebout, Janice C. May, Thomas A. Morehouse, and Victor Fischer. Preparation and publication of the book would not have been possible without the help of Guy Van Doren and Landa Krossa, staff of the Alaska Legislature; Lee Gorsuch, director of the Institute of Social and Economic Research; and Ron Crowe, editor of ISER publications. Financial support for the project was provided by the Joint Committee on the Constitutional Convention; Representative Brian Rogers, Chairman; and the Senate State Affairs Committee, Senator Victor Fischer, Chairman.

Gordon S. Harrison
March 1982

Table of Contents

Foreword iii
Acknowledgments.................................... viii
Table of Contents ix
Introduction 1
  What is a State Constitution? 2
  The Background of Alaska's Constitution 3
    Statehood Movement 4
    Territorial Experience 5
    Lack of Institutional Development 6
    Contemporary Constitutional Theory 6
    The State Constitutional Reform Movement 7

Article I. Declaration of Rights 9
Article II. The Legislature 21
Article III. The Executive 35
Article IV. The Judiciary 45
Article V. Suffrage and Elections 53
Article VI. Legislative Apportionment 57
Article VII. Health, Education, and Welfare 63
Article VIII. Natural Resources 67
Article IX. Finance and Taxation 77
Article X. Local Government 85
Article XI. The Initiative, Referendum, and Recall 93
Article XII. General Provisions 101
Article XIII. Amendment and Revision 107
Article XV. Schedule of Transitional Measures 113

Appendices

Appendix A. List of All Constitutional Amendments
  through 1980 116
Appendix B. Article XIV. Apportionment Schedule 118
Appendix C. Article XV. Schedule of Transitional Measures 125

Introduction

At the general election in 1982, Alaskans will vote on the question: "Shall there be a constitutional convention?" If a majority votes "yes," a convention will meet to examine Alaska's constitution and prepare changes to it that will be submitted to the voters for ratification.

Does Alaska's constitution need to be examined by a convention? This is a question voters must answer for themselves. Before making up their minds, many will want to know more about our constitution. What does it say? How well has it worked for the first 20 years of statehood? What amendments have been made so far? How has the state supreme court interpreted its various provisions?

The purpose of *A Citizen's Guide to Alaska's Constitution* is to help answer these questions. This book discusses the origin and evolution of Alaska's constitution. It introduces the general subject matter of each article and explains how the delegates to Alaska's first constitutional convention approached the major issues which the subject raised. Then each section of the article is presented together with commentary that touches on key ideas, words, phrases, concepts, usages, and judicial interpretations. At times little or no comment is necessary. But often a brief discussion is necessary to provide a measure of perspective for the reader who is only casually acquainted with Alaska's constitution and recent political history.

In short, this is a guided tour through Alaska's basic law. It is written for the citizen who wants to learn more about Alaska's constitution.

What is a State Constitution?

State constitutions create the framework of government in each of the fifty states. This framework is basically the same in all states. It involves a system of government with three branches: a legislative branch, typically composed of two chambers; an executive branch, with its numerous administrative agencies; and a judicial branch, with a supreme court and a system of lower courts. Each branch is largely independent of the others, but there are mutual checks and balances that prevent the concentration of too much power in one branch. This framework of state government is designed to limit the power of government in order to protect the liberties of citizens.

This basic system of state government dates from the American revolutionary period when the thirteen colonies created independent constitutional governments. We recognize the system as the one embodied in the federal constitution, which was an amalgam of ideas and political principles expressed in the constitutions of the thirteen original states. The federal constitution was written in 1787 when it became apparent to the citizens of the thirteen states that a strong central government was necessary for economic prosperity and military defense. The U.S. Constitution delegated certain powers to the new federal government and reserved others for the states. It also prohibited the federal government from violating basic personal rights and political freedoms.

While all state governments follow the general pattern established by the revolutionary states and the federal government, they vary widely in the details of structure and operation. For example, Nebraska has only one legislative chamber, whereas all of the other states have two. Alaska has a total of sixty members in its legislature (20 senators and 40 representatives), whereas New Hampshire has 424. The heads of many executive departments are elected individually in some states, while they are appointed by the governor in others (Alaska included). Also, many state schemes exist for selecting and removing judges. In sum, there are many interesting, important differences among state governments.

State constitutions also vary a great deal from state to state. Some documents are quite long and burdened with detail, while others are short and general. These characteristics depend upon the historical period in which the constitutions were written and the unique social and political experience of the individual states. Alaska is among the states with a short constitution. It speaks only to the broad principles of governmental organization and operation and leaves the details of implementation to the legislature.

As a general rule, long and detailed constitutions need frequent amendment. This is because they attempt to describe the minutiae of governmental structure, procedures, and public policy. The political, social, and economic life of society changes; and when an existing detail of government becomes obsolete or a new one needs to be created, it is usually necessary to amend these constitutions. Thus, short, general constitutions tend to be more flexible in the face of change. They allow the legislature and courts more leeway to adapt general constitutional principles to conditions unforeseen by the drafters of the original document.

Courts have historically played a major role in adapting constitutional language to changing social and economic conditions. It is the duty of the courts to interpret the constitution when cases come before them that raise constitutional questions. This is one way that general constitutional language comes to have specific meaning. (Thus it is necessary to refer often to state supreme court decisions in this survey of Alaska's constitution.) In their interpretation of constitutional provisions, the state courts may find that a law passed by the legislature or by a local government, or an action of a governmental agency, is contrary to the meaning of the constitution and therefore cannot be enforced.

This practice of determining the constitutionality of laws and administrative acts is called judicial review. The federal courts can declare the laws of Congress or of the states unconstitutional. Judicial review is profoundly important in our system of constitutional government even though there is no mention of it in the U.S. Constitution. One consequence of judicial review by the federal courts is that state constitutional provisions can also be nullified if they conflict with the federal constitution. This is because the U.S. Constitution is the "supreme law of the land" and therefore superior to state consitutions as well as acts of Congress and the executive branch, state governments, and local governments.

A great deal more could be said about the theory, operation, and history of constitutions in the United States, but there is not space for it here. However, the following analysis of Alaska's constitution is intended to help provide an understanding of the general principles of constitutional government, as well as provide an explanation of the origin and implementation of Alaska's specific constitutional language.

The Background of Alaska's Constitution

Alaska's constitution creates a system of government that is fundamentally similar to that of the other states. It is nevertheless a unique document. Alaska's constitution gives expression to traditional American ideals and political forms, but it does so in its own historical context. Therefore, our examination of the constitution must begin with the constitutional convention of 1955-1956 and the dominant social, economic, and political influences of that time. These include the statehood movement, the experience of territorial government, the lack of institutional development in the territory, and contemporary constitutional theory.

Statehood Movement

That the constitution was produced as part of the statehood movement had important influence on the document, although it is not possible to explain this significance by pointing to specific provisions, language, or subject matter in the constitution. The Alaska constitution was written in the winter of 1955-56 at the University of Alaska, Fairbanks (an academic setting was thought to encourage reflective deliberation). Statehood was still 3 years away, and at the time the prospects did not seem good for Congress to grant Alaska statehood. The constitutional convention was conceived as a tactical maneuver in the battle for statehood. Many Alaskans hoped that a good constitution written and acclaimed by the people of the territory would help promote their cause.

Delegates to the constitutional convention were, for the most part, enthusiastic proponents of statehood. They shared the idealism, dedication, and brotherhood of the long statehood movement; and they brought to their deliberations a high spirit of public purpose, consensus, and camaraderie. Absent from the convention was a faction openly opposed to statehood—a group who feared the creation of new state governmental authority and the taxes and regulations which would inevitably follow. Nor were there those present who sought to protect their own economic interests by perpetuating the existing absentee system of federal bureaucratic administration. This general unanimity of outlook did not mean that all the delegates saw everything the same way or that differences of opinion went unargued. It did mean, however, that compromises could be easily reached when disputes arose, and that the convention was spared deep, bitter, divisive conflict over basic policy issues.

Because the new constitution was to be used to help sell Congress on the statehood idea, delegates were mindful of its public-relations value. Through this document and its preparation, Alaskans sought to demonstrate to Congress that they possessed political maturity and a capability for self-government. This consideration further encouraged convention delegates to compromise their differences (which often meant postponing the resolution of disputes by handing the matters to the future legislature). The desire to demonstrate political maturity discouraged the use of brazen bargaining and obstructionist parliamentary tactics often present in such gatherings. Statehood considerations also encouraged the delegates to (1) adopt a short and general document similar to that of the United States Constitution; (2) employ the most up-to-date and progressive notions of constitutional draftsmanship; (3) make use of political symbolism (for example, there were fifty-five delegates to the convention, the same number that met in Philadelphia in 1798); and (4) be impeccably democratic in their procedures (the convention itself was the most representative body in the history of the territory).

The statehood movement also influenced the constitution by orienting it to the *future* development of the state. Alaskans envisioned rapid growth and development of their state once they possessed the means of self-government. U.S. Supreme Court Justice Benjamin Cardozo once wrote that a good constitution states "not the rules for the passing hour but principles for an expanding future." Alaska's constitution was intended to accommodate an expanding future. One way it did this was through its broad, uncomplicated grants of power to the legislature; thus a keen awareness of the future helped the convention delegates create a flexible document.

Territorial Experience

A strong governor and a strong legislature are dominant features of Alaska's state government, and these reflect a reaction to the weaknesses of Alaska's governmental institutions during the territorial period. When Alaska was granted territorial status in 1912, a legislature was authorized. However, Congress limited its powers and retained control over matters of vital interest to the residents of the territory. Congress, for example, restricted the legislative power to raise revenue through bonding and taxation. It also withheld from the legislature responsibility for management of the territory's commercial fish and minerals. Executive authority in the territory was similarly weak and ineffective. The governor and secretary of state were federal appointees, and administrative rulemaking and authority were dispersed among many independent boards and commissions.

This territorial scheme partly reflected the notion in Washington, D.C. that Alaska was too remote and too sparsely settled to warrant a greater measure of self-government. However, it also served the interests of federal bureaucracies with long-standing jurisdiction over Alaska's resources, as well as the interests of absentee corporations that exploited these resources. Here the issue was mainly the management of Alaska's fisheries, which were dominated by Seattle and San Francisco canning interests, and Alaska's mineral industries, which were dominated by major East Coast corporations. Alaskans long suspected a silent conspiracy between the bureaucratic managers and the corporate interests; they considered the weak, poor, and decentralized territorial government a result of that conspiracy.

It is not surprising that when crafting their own charter for self-government, Alaska's constitutional convention delegates created extraordinarily strong legislative and executive branches of government. This meant avoiding limitations, prohibitions, and debilitating hedges on the power of the legislature to act; and it meant avoiding the diffusion of executive power through boards, commissions, and numerous elected officials. These principles of legislative and executive organization were considered necessary to make government effective, accountable to the public, and free from the grip of special interests. While they were compromised somewhat in the final document, these ideals guided the delegates in their work.

Lack of Institutional Development

At the time of the constitutional convention, Alaska was much more sparsely settled and undeveloped than it is now. Such a lack of development meant the state was also *institutionally* undeveloped. Delegates to the constitutional convention did not have to contend with entrenched local political jurisdictions, court systems, or other established authorities typical of more populous states. The delegates were largely free to structure a rational system of government from their own ideas and theories of representative government. Indeed, the comparative lack of established institutions at the time of the convention invited innovation by the delegates. For example, the delegates had the opportunity to design a system of local government for Alaska before most areas of the state required local government. In contrast, elsewhere in the United States the movement to reform metropolitan area government was hopelessly stalled by the defensive reaction of the many existing local governmental units and special service districts.

Contemporary Constitutional Theory

Alaska's constitution was written by territorial residents who reflected the unique political aspirations and experience of Alaskans. However, there is nothing parochial about the document. Indeed it embodies the most modern and progressive concepts of state constitutional draftsmanship. The delegates were aware of the current thinking of political scientists and state constitutional lawyers. They hired several experts from around the country to advise them, and they had at hand the "Model State Constitution" prepared by the National Municipal League. Contemporary theory matched well the ideas and inclinations of the Alaska delegates, but we cannot overlook the influence of this body of academic opinion on the shape of the final document. For example, much of the language used in the constitution was taken directly from the League's model constitution.

The State Constitutional Reform Movement

In the late 1930s there emerged an active constitutional reform movement in the United States. The role of government in society had expanded tremendously in the first part of the 20th century, and many states found their constitutions standing in the path of progress. These long, complicated documents were typically the product of the nineteenth century and its popular distrust of politicians and government from smoke-filled rooms. Legislative and executive authority were often intentionally crippled by constitutional reservations, limitations and prohibitions; by the dispersal of governmental power; and by deliberate inefficiencies in governmental operation. In the face of new demands for governmental services, lawmakers had to turn again and again to the cumbersome and uncertain process of amendment to escape these constitutional strictures.

The constitutional reform movement stressed the need to simplify and shorten state constitutions; rid them of statutory detail, leaving only fundamental material; and unshackle the legislature and governor's office so they could conduct their business more efficiently. This reform movement came to be centered in the National Municipal League, headquartered in New York City. A major contribution of the League was publication of the *Model State Constitution*, which represented the combined efforts at constitutional reform of political scientists, lawyers, and practitioners of government at the state and local levels. Underlying the state constitutional reform movement was a positive belief in the potential of government to solve contemporary problems. This view is expressed well in the introduction of a League publication:

> The authors of this volume are not joining the chorus of those who bemoan the expansion of governmental activity in this country. They appre-

ciate the role that government can play in the solution of our social problems, in the raising of our standard of living and in securing the blessings of liberty...[1]

Delegates to the constitutional convention also viewed state government as a potentially positive force in the social and economic development of Alaska. They were confident in the wisdom and dedication of their fellow citizens to govern for the common good. They saw how special interests thrived in the absence of strong political authority, and they wanted to reassert the public interest. In sum, the reigning notions of good constitutional government were well received by the convention at Fairbanks in the winter of 1955-56.

The Alaska constitution begins with this preamble:

We the people of Alaska, grateful to God and to those who founded our nation and pioneered this great land, in order to secure and transmit to succeeding generations our heritage of political, civil, and religious liberty within the United States, do ordain and establish this constitution for the State of Alaska.

The following pages present the Alaska Constitution and brief commentary on its major provisions.

---

[1]John P. Wheeler, Ed., *Salient Issues of Constitutional Revision*, National Municipal League, New York, 1961.

Article I
Declaration of Rights

All state constitutions contain a declaration of rights. Most of these, like Alaska's, follow closely the Bill of Rights in the U.S. Constitution. Personal rights protected by the federal and state constitutions are basic to our political system, for they guarantee to every citizen civil and political freedoms that we consider necessary for human liberty. It is often said that the essence of constitutional government is limited government, because constitutional protection of basic human rights limits the scope of governmental power. Although the abuses of authority that gave rise to many of these rights have now largely disappeared from this country, we need only look at the excesses of totalitarian and dictatorial governments in the world around us to be reminded of how important these rights still are.

While the delegates to Alaska's constitutional convention were willing to innovate when they saw the need for innovation (for example in the articles dealing with local government and natural resources), they saw no need to venture far from the time-honored phrases of the federal constitution when drafting a declaration of rights for their new state. The statement of rights in the U.S. Constitution had served the country well, and decades of judicial usage had given practical meaning to the language (including such phrases as "due process of law"). In addition, the delegates avoided unnecessary innovation because they could never be sure of the ultimate legal interpretation of new language they might invent, and new terms and legal concepts they might adopt could require years of judicial application to clarify.

Also, in selecting rights to enshrine in the new state constitution, and in phrasing these rights, the convention delegates were mindful of the symbolic functions of the document. Alaskans would beseech Congress for statehood with this document as proof of their political maturity and evidence of a shared political heritage. And, of course, the constitution was to symbolize governmental authority for Alaska's citizenry. Therefore, the delegates sought to express the nobility of the American democratic tradition with words and concepts drawn directly from documents of our political history.

This is not to say that Alaska's declaration of rights is a carbon copy of the federal Bill of Rights. The delegates did rearrange, restate, expand, and embellish the rights found in the U.S. Constitution to some extent. While they retained the essence of these rights and most of the original wording in the Alaska Constitution, the delegates often modified wording of the rights to account for contemporary circumstances and the perspective gained from over 150 years of interpretation.

Ironically, the Alaska electorate has shown itself much more willing to expand upon the traditional statement of personal liberties than was the constitutional convention. Indeed, Alaskans have been less timid in this respect than the voters and the courts at the national level. In 1972, Alaska voters approved two constitutional amendments to Article I. One adds the word "sex" to Section 3, which now states: "No person is to be denied the enjoyment of any civil or political right because of race, color, creed, sex, or national origin." The other creates an explicit right of privacy. A new section, number 22, was appended to Article I which states: "The right of the people to privacy is recognized and shall not be infringed." It remains to be seen how these new constitutional rights will actually enlarge the substance of existing rights derived from such traditional guarantees as equal protection of the laws and prohibition of unreasonable searches and seizures.

In its interpretation of new and traditional rights, Alaska's supreme court can never provide a degree of protection below that provided by the United States Supreme Court under the federal constitution. The fourteenth amendment to the federal constitution, adopted in 1868, has gradually come to be interpreted to apply virtually all of the Bill of Rights to the states. Thus, the basic civil rights of a citizen would be protected by the federal consitution even if the state did not have its own constitutional declaration of rights. In a strict legal sense, therefore, it may not have been necessary to repeat many of the provisions of the federal constitution in Alaska's constitution. However, in its application of Alaska's own constitutional guarantees, the state supreme court may broaden and diversify the protection that a state citizen might enjoy under federal law. Alaska's supreme court justices have declared, "We are not limited by decisions of the U.S. Supreme Court or the U.S. Constitution when we expound our state constitution; the Alaska constitution may have broader safeguards than the minimum federal standards" (Roberts v. State, 458 P.2d 340; 1969).

Thus, the declaration of rights in Alaska's constitution, though traditional in most respects, is a unique and independent source of political liberty for citizens of our state.

Section 1. Inherent Rights

> This constitution is dedicated to the principles that all persons have a natural right to life, liberty, the pursuit of happiness, and the enjoyment of the rewards of their own industry; that all persons are equal and entitled to equal rights, opportunities, and protection under the law; and that all persons have corresponding obligations to the people and to the State.

These words have the ring of a preamble (which is not, in a legal sense, a working part of a constitution). However, the section is a substantive part of the constitution and the courts have found it to contain legally enforceable rights. The key phrase is "All persons are . . . entitled to equal rights, opportunities, and protection under the law." This language follows the fourteenth amendment to the U.S. Constitution, which prohibits states from denying any person "equal protection of the laws." This fundamental principle has been interpreted very broadly over the years by the U.S. Supreme Court. It now means that people and organizations may not be treated differently unless there is compelling reason to do so. Thus, for example, difference in treatment based on the color of one's skin is illegal.

The last phrase, "All persons have corresponding obligations to the people and to the state," is novel and has yet had no specific legal application or interpretation.

Section 2. Source of Government

> All political power is inherent in the people. All government originates with the people, is founded upon their will only, and is instituted solely for the good of the people as a whole.

Here again are preamble-like passages. The section states the theory of democratic institutions which we recognize as derived from the Declaration of Independence and the U.S. Constitution. So far, the courts have not found a practical application of it. However, an Alaska attorney general's opinion states that this section would prevent the government from banning write-in voting, for example.

Section 3. Civil Rights

> No person is to be denied the enjoyment of any civil or political right because of race, color, creed, sex, or national origin. The legislature shall implement this section.

The word "sex" in the first sentence in this section was added by amendment in 1972. Whether or not to include this word in the original language was hotly debated at the constitutional convention, but it was omitted—ironically, by the persuasion of a female delegate who argued that the rights of women had been and would continue to be protected by Alaska's legislature.

This section makes explicit the prohibitions against discrimination that are implied in the "equal protection" provision of Section 1. The legislature has implemented the broad protection of this section as directed to do so in the second sentence. Chapter 80 in Title 18 of the Alaska Statutes spells out in detail unlawful discriminatory practices in employment, public accommodations, the sale and rental of housing, financing, and governmental operations. The statutes also establish a State Commission on Human Rights with power to investigate formal complaints of discrimination and to order a remedy for violation of the law.

Section 4. Freedom of Religion

> No law shall be made respecting an establishment of religion, or prohibiting the free exercise thereof.

An interesting interpretation of this familiar American constitutional guarantee occurred recently in Alaska. The state supreme court said that an Athabascan Indian funeral potlatch was a religious ritual, and that a participant could not be prosecuted for killing a moose out of season which was consumed at the gathering (Frank v. State, 604 P.2d 1068; 1979).

Section 5. Freedom of Speech

> Every person may freely speak, write, and publish on all subjects, being responsible for the abuse of that right.

The convention delegates selected this wording from the Idaho constitution, preferring it to the more dramatic but perhaps too sweeping language of the first amendment of the federal constitution ("Congress shall make no law abridging the freedom of speech, or of the press"). The curious clause "being responsible for the abuse of that right" recognizes, as the courts have long recognized, that the freedom to speak and publish are not absolute. These rights may be restrained to protect a legitimate public interest, such as discouraging libel.

Section 6. Assembly; Petition

> The right of the people peaceably to assemble, and to petition the government shall never be abridged.

This language is derived directly from the first amendment of the U.S. Constitution. No cases have yet reached the Alaska supreme court which allege a violation of this fundamental political freedom.

Section 7. Due Process

> No person shall be deprived of life, liberty, or property, without due process of law. The right of all persons to fair and just treatment in the course of legislative and executive investigations shall not be infringed.

Here the famous "due process" clause of the Bill of Rights is enshrined in the Alaska constitution. Through decades of decisions, the courts have given this clause a very broad and expansive meaning. It does not simply mean that the legislature must pass a law before it deprives someone of life, liberty, or property. The clause has been elevated to a prominent principle of justice and fair play that may never be violated by any branch of government.

The convention delegates incorporated novel language in this section by explicitly extending the due-process principle to legislative and executive investigations. This was done in reaction to the blustering anticommunist investigations of Senator Joseph McCarthy in the mid-1950s that offended the public's sense of fair treatment by the government.

Section 8. Grand Jury

> No person shall be held to answer for a capital, or otherwise infamous crime, unless on a presentment or indictment of a grand jury, except in cases arising in the armed forces in time of war or public danger. Indictment may be waived by the accused. In that case the prosecution shall be by information. The grand jury shall consist of at least twelve citizens, a majority of whom concurring may return an indictment. The power of grand juries to investigate and make recommendations concerning the public welfare or safety shall never be suspended.

The issue of the grand jury caused a measure of controversy at the constitutional convention, and it has continued to be a source of controversy in Alaska since. This section adopts for Alaska the use of the grand jury in serious state criminal cases. The U.S. Bill of Rights requires indictments by a grand jury in federal felony cases, but the U.S. Supreme Court has held that this federal procedure does not apply to the states via the fourteenth amendment. Thus, states are not required to use the grant jury procedure; about one-half, including Alaska, have chosen to do so.

The grand jury is a device to ensure that the government does not bring frivolous and arbitrary criminal charges against a person.

Before anyone can be put on trial for a high federal crime, a grand jury of unbiased citizens must fairly consider the evidence against the accused person. An indictment, or formal accusation, is thus issued by the grand jury, not the prosecutor. The grand jury, like the rest of our legal institutions, is rooted in the deep history of English jurisprudence.

Delegates at the constitutional convention decided to incorporate the grand jury procedure into state criminal procedures. However, they made an exception. The grand jury system had an unusual problem in Alaska during territorial days. In smaller towns the grand jury might sit for only a few weeks each year. A person charged with a serious crime soon after it adjourned might have to wait for most of a year before a new grand jury would convene to decide on indictment. Even if the accused person went free on bail in the meantime, the wait was unreasonable and conflicted with his right to a speedy trial. The delegates dealt with this problem in the constitution with the language that allows a person charged with a serious crime under state law to waive his or her right to indictment by a grand jury and be formally charged by the prosecutor (in which case the prosecution is by "information") if the accused person wants to get on with the matter.

Critics of the grand jury argue that it is an archaic procedure that no longer serves a real purpose. There are in our system of law today other procedural and professional safeguards that prevent the abuses of official power that the grand jury is supposed to prevent. Therefore, some people who are familiar with the working of the court system believe it could be streamlined without reducing protection for the citizen by eliminating the grand jury process and replacing it with one of several less cumbersome alternative indictment procedures.

Section 9. Jeopardy and Self-Incrimination

> No person shall be put in jeopardy twice for the same offense. No person shall be compelled in any criminal proceeding to be a witness against himself.

This section states long-established principles of Anglo-American law that no person may be tried twice for the same crime, and that an accused person has the right to remain silent in the face of criminal accusations.

Section 10. Treason

> Treason against the State consists only in levying war against it, or in adhering to its enemies, giving them aid and comfort. No person

> shall be convicted of treason, unless on the testimony of two witnesses to the same overt act, or on confession in open court.

This language, taken from Article III, Section 3 of the federal constitution, defines treason and establishes the minimum evidence required to support a conviction.

Section 11. Rights of Accused

> In all criminal prosecutions, the accused shall have the right to a speedy and public trial, by an impartial jury of twelve, except that the legislature may provide for a jury of not more than twelve nor less than six in courts not of record. The accused is entitled to be informed of the nature and cause of the accusation; to be released on bail, except for capital offenses when the proof is evident or the presumption great; to be confronted with the witnesses against him; to have compulsory process for obtaining witnesses in his favor, and to have the assistance of counsel for his defense.

These are basic procedural safeguards that are established in the sixth article of the U.S. Bill of Rights. Alaska's provision differs from the federal constitution in that it allows the legislature to provide for a jury of from six to twelve people in courts "not of record"—that is, in the district courts. Exercising this discretion, the legislature has designated that these juries are to consist of six members (A.S. 22.15.150).

There have been several attempts in the legislature over the years to amend the bail provisions of this section. These efforts have sought to limit the right of bail by repeated criminal offenders.

Section 12. Excessive Punishment

> Excessive bail shall not be required, nor excessive fines imposed, nor cruel and unusual punishments inflicted. Penal administration shall be based on the principle of reformation and upon the need for protecting the public.

The first sentence of this section states basic principles of justice which are firmly established in American law. The second sentence expresses the progressive view of imprisonment—one familiar to us but not found in the U.S. Constitution. There have been unsuccessful resolutions introduced in the legislature to amend this language to give judges the grounds to impose harsh, punitive sentences on criminals, particularly those whose crimes include violence. For its part, the state supreme court has interpreted expansively the second sentence of Section 12 to include four sentencing goals: *rehabilitation* of the offender, *isolation* of the offender from society, *deterrence* of the offender and others disposed to commit similar acts, and community *condemnation* of the offense. However, the court has ruled that sentencing for retribution is inconsistent with this section (State v. Chaney, 477 P.2d 441; 1970).

Section 13. Habeas Corpus

> The privilege of the writ of habeas corpus shall not be suspended, unless when in cases of rebellion or actual or imminent invasion, the public safety requires it.

The writ of *habeas corpus* is a judicial means of preventing a person from being jailed without cause. It is perhaps the oldest and most famous safeguard of personal liberty in the Anglo-American judicial tradition. The U.S. Constitution protects the writ in Article I, Section 9.

Section 14. Searches and Seizures

> The right of the people to be secure in their persons, houses and other property, papers, and effects, against unreasonable searches and seizures, shall not be violated. No warrants shall issue, but upon probable cause, supported by oath or affirmation, and particularly describing the place to be searched, and the persons or things to be seized.

Here is stated word for word the search-and-seizure article of the U.S. Bill of Rights. At the Alaska constitutional convention, the delegates seriously considered, but finally rejected, an additional clause that would have extended this principle to include freedom from unlawful electronic surveillance and wiretapping. It was decided that the legislature would deal adequately with serious problems of this type if they occurred.

Section 15. Prohibited State Action

> No bill of attainder or ex post facto law shall be passed. No law impairing the obligation of contracts, and no law making any irrevocable grant of special privileges or immunities shall be passed. No conviction shall work corruption of blood or forfeiture of estate.

This section reaffirms the explicit prohibitions on state action found in Article I, Section 10 of the U.S. Constitution. A bill of attainder is an act of the legislature that singles out a person for punishment and makes a determination of the person's guilt. (Such a determination is the proper role of the courts in our society, not the legislature.) Only rarely in the history of our country have there been bills of attainder. One such case occurred in Alaska. A powerful member of the senate finance committee inserted a rider in the 1980 appropriation bill that eliminated the position control number (a state personnel number assigned to an individual) belonging to an agency administrator whom the senator wanted removed. The attorney general advised the governor to ignore the rider because it was legislative punishment of a named person and therefore amounted to a bill of attainder.

An *ex post facto* law is one that makes certain acts a crime that were innocent at the time they were committed. The phrase "irrevocable grant of special privileges or immunities" substitutes for "titles of nobility" in the federal version. This substitute language is found in many state constitutions. It may reflect a reaction to corrupt nineteenth century legislatures giving preferences and exclusive rights to corporations such as railroads.

The last sentence is not found in the U.S. Constitution but states the recognized principle that conviction of a crime should not affect one's family ("the sins of the father should not be visited upon his children") or rights to property legitimately acquired.

Section 16. Civil Suits; Trial by Jury

> In civil cases where the amount in controversy exceeds two hundred fifty dollars, the right of trial by a jury of twelve is preserved to the same extent as it existed at common law. The legislature may make provision for a verdict by not less than three-fourths of the jury and, in courts not of record, may provide for a jury of not less than six or more than twelve.

This language is derived from the Bill of Rights. However, a measure of flexibility is written into the state constitution in the second sentence that does not appear in the U.S. Constitution. The legislature has decided not to allow a verdict on less than a unanimous vote of the jury, but it has provided for a jury of six in the district courts.

Section 17. Imprisonment for Debt

> There shall be no imprisonment for debt. This section does not prohibit civil arrest of absconding debtors.

A provision similar to this is not found in the U.S. Constitution but is included in several state constitutions. It means that a person who is in debt may not be put in jail, but the person may be punished if he flees deliberately to avoid paying his debts.

Section 18. Eminent Domain

> Private property shall not be taken or damaged for public use without just compensation.

The right of eminent domain, that is, the right to take private property for a public purpose, is a traditional exercise of state power. This section emphasizes that the state must pay a fair value for the property when exercising that right (see also Article VIII, Section 18).

Section 19. Right to Bear Arms
> A well-regulated militia being necessary to the security of a free state, the right of the people to keep and bear arms shall not be infringed.

Courts have ruled that this language, which comes from the U.S. Bill of Rights, does not prevent Congress or the states from regulating private ownership of guns, as long as the regulation does not interfere with the state militia (national guard).

Section 20. Quartering Soldiers
> No member of the armed forces shall in time of peace be quartered in any house without the consent of the owner or occupant, or in time of war except as prescribed by law. The military shall be in strict subordination to the civil power.

This obsolete provision is derived from the federal constitution. Its inclusion in the Alaska constitution reveals the strong influence of tradition on the convention delegates.

Section 21. Construction
> The enumeration of rights in this constitution shall not impair or deny others retained by the people.

Although Article I may omit mention of other rights, enjoyment of those rights is not denied to the people. This is a principle recognized by the Bill of Rights.

Section 22. Right of Privacy
> The right of the people to privacy is recognized and shall not be infringed. The legislature shall implement this section.

This entire section was added to the constitution by amendment in 1972. It recognizes a right to privacy that is implied in other constitutional guarantees (freedom from unreasonable search and seizure, and due process of law, for examples) but which the courts have never formally recognized as a free-standing right. What the new right really means is not yet clear. It may be many years before the state supreme court fully delineates the range of citizen activity that is protected from governmental interference by this provision. The presumption is, however, that something more is protected by this right than by existing rights because otherwise it would be meaningless. So far, the state supreme court has moved cautiously. It has not seized upon the right of privacy to drive government from areas it has long regulated. Nonetheless, the court did declare that this constitutional right does allow a citizen of Alaska to possess marijuana for personal use (Ravin v. State, 537 P.2d 494; 1975).

Article II
The Legislature

The legislature is one of three branches of government in the American constitutional system. This system is built around the twin doctrines of "separation of powers" and "checks and balances." Separation of powers refers to the principle that the three functions of government—legislative, executive, and judicial—should be performed by separate and coequal bodies. Checks and balances refers to exceptions to the separation of powers which are authorized by the constitution or sanctioned by tradition. These exceptions prevent the concentration of excessive power in one branch of government. Thus, under the separation of powers doctrine, the legislature makes laws, the executive implements them, and the judiciary interprets and enforces them when necessary. However, under the principle of checks and balances, the constitution authorizes the executive to exercise certain functions in the legislative and judicial areas, such as vetoing bills passed by the legislature and appointing judges; the legislature to exercise certain functions in the executive and judicial areas, such as approving apointments to major executive departments and exercising veto power over procedural court rules; and the judiciary to exercise oversight over legislative and administrative actions to insure their conformity with the laws and constitution of the state.[2] One consequence of this arrangement is an inherent tension between the three branches of government as each guards against encroachments on its power by the others.

Article II vests the legislative power of the state in the legislature; provides the basic structure, composition, and procedures of

---

[2]The power of judicial review which allows the courts to nullify an act of the legislature derives from an unwritten constitutional principle. It was first enunciated by the U.S. Supreme Court in the historic case of Marbury v. Madison in 1803.

the legislature; and specifies the main legislative power (the veto) which may be exercised by the governor. When the convention delegates wrote Alaska's constitution, they sought to create a strong legislature with the power and resources to act decisively and effectively. The delegates assumed that the legislature would always act responsibly.

While many state constitutions reflect profound suspicion of the legislature, Alaska's constitution declares confidence and trust in the legislative body. The legislature is comparatively small in size; there is no limit on the length of its sessions; it meets annually; its members are paid a salary; and it may arrange for its own supporting services. A major expression of confidence in the legislature is the broad discretion the constitution gives it to fashion the details of government structure and operation (details which are specified in the constitution of many states).

However, legislative action is not altogether unrestrained by the constitution. For example, there are safeguards against intrusion by the legislature in local affairs and against borrowing money for capital projects without the voters' approval. While the delegates may not have worried about the development of legislative tyranny, they nonetheless thought it prudent to erect barriers to legislative exuberance.

Section 1. Legislative Power; Membership
> The legislative power of the State is vested in a legislature consisting of a senate with a membership of twenty and a house of representatives with a membership of forty.

Here a bicameral (two-house) legislature is created with twenty senators and forty representatives. The alternative to a bicameral legislature is a one-house (unicameral) legislature. Only one state, Nebraska, has a unicameral legislature. At the convention, this alternative sparked a lively debate, but there was never enough support for the idea to be seriously considered for adoption. It is interesting to note, however, that Alaska's constitution is unique in its frequent use of joint legislative sessions. For example, joint sessions are required for the confirmation of executive appointments, overriding vetos, and other purposes (see, for example, Article II, Section 16; Article III, Sections 19, 20, 23, 25, and 26; Article IV, Sections 8 and 10; in contrast, see Article X, Section 12). Frequent use of joint sessions may reflect a residual interest in the unicameral concept on the part of the convention delegates.

Alaska's voters have flirted with the unicameral concept. In 1976, proponents of a unicameral legislature placed an initiative proposition on the statewide ballot which was intended to "advise" the legislature of their desire to consider a constitutional amendment to create a unicameral legislature. (Constitutional amendments cannot be proposed directly by the initiative process; see discussion of Article XIII.) The proposition passed, but the legislature has not pursued the matter. This should surprise no one, since the senate is not about to abolish itself even if the members of the lower house believe unicameralism is a good idea (although in 1978, a unicameral amendment did not pass the house). If a constitutional amendment to achieve unicameralism is ever to reach the voters, it will have to be proposed by a constitutional convention.

At sixty members, Alaska's legislature is among the smallest in the United States. The smaller the number of legislators, the greater the relative power and prestige of each. The size of Alaska's legislature was thoroughly debated at the consitutional convention, but it has not been a serious political question since. However, proposed amendments have appeared from time to time in the legislature that would change the membership of each house to an odd number to eliminate the possibility of tie votes. None of these has passed.

Section 2. Members: Qualifications

> A member of the legislature shall be a qualified voter who has been a resident of Alaska for at least three years and of the district from which elected for at least one year, immediately preceding his filing for office. A senator shall be at least twenty-five years of age and a representative at least twenty-one years of age.

These qualifications for holding legislative office are typical of those in most states. A candidate for the senate in Alaska once challenged these requirements, arguing that they abridged his rights of equal protection and petition of the government. Usually hostile to residency requirements, the state supreme court upheld the requirements in this case, stating that three years of residency served a legitimate interest in insuring that legislators had resided in the state long enough to understand its history, geography, needs, and problems. Further, the court ruled that the one-year residency requirement in the election district is appropriate in order to permit constituents to recognize, understand, and talk with those who seek public office (Gilbert v. State, 526 P.2d 1131; 1974).

Section 3. Election and Terms

> Legislators shall be elected at general elections. Their terms begin on the fourth Monday of the January following election unless otherwise provided by law. The term of representatives shall be two years, and the term of senators, four years. One-half of the senators shall be elected every two years.

A two-year term for representatives is the standard in all but four states; a four-year term for senators is the standard in all but twelve. Therefore, Alaska may be considered typical in its length of legislative terms. In 1975, the legislature exercised its discretion to set the first day of these terms. The law now specifies: "The term of each member of the legislature begins on the second Monday in January following a presidential election year; however, following a gubernatorial election year, the term of each member begins on the third Monday in January."

Section 4. Vacancies

> A vacancy in the legislature shall be filled for the unexpired term as provided by law. If no provision is made, the governor shall fill the vacancy by appointment.

According to legislative provisions for filling a vacancy, the governor makes an appointment which must be confirmed by the house or senate caucus (a caucus is a group of legislators who belong to the same political party or faction) to which the predecessor belonged. A special election is called when a vacancy occurs in the senate which leaves an unexpired term of more than two years, five months. The full details of these provisions are found in A.S. 40.320-470.

Section 5. Disqualifications

> No legislator may hold any other office or position of profit under the United States or the State. During the term for which elected and for one year thereafter, no legislator may be nominated, elected, or appointed to any other office or position of profit which has been created, or the salary or emoluments of which have been increased, while he was a member. This section shall not prevent any person from seeking or holding the office of governor, secretary of state, or member of Congress. This section shall not apply to employment by or election to a constitutional convention.

This section is an effort by the framers of the constitution to keep legislators from situations where their loyalties might conflict and their good judgment be compromised as a result. The first sentence is a prohibition against dual office holding. The rationale for this prohibition has been explained by the state supreme court as an effort "to guard against conflicts of interest, self-aggrandizement, concentration of power, and dilution of separation of powers. . . ." (Begich v. Jefferson, 441 P.2d 27; 1968). This provision has been literally applied by the state supreme court. For example, a teacher working for the state had to resign his job before he could serve in the legislature.

The second sentence prohibits a legislator from creating an office in which to serve, or increasing the salary of a job he hopes to get. The supreme court has said that this provision of the constitution is designed not merely to prevent an individual legislator from profiting by an action taken by him with bad motives, but to prevent all legislators from being influenced by either conscious or unconscious motives (Warwick v. State Ex Rel Chance, 548 P.2d 384; 1976).

The provision does not, in the opinion of the attorney general, prevent a member of one house running for a seat in the other house even if legislative salaries have increased.

In times when salary adjustments are frequent, this provision effectively bars all legislators from state employment for a year after their legislative service. In 1980, a proposed amendment to the constitution was put before the voters that would have eliminated this provision of Section 5, but it was defeated.

Section 6. Immunities

> Legislators may not be held to answer before any other tribunal for any statement made in the exercise of their legislative duties while the legislature is in session. Members attending, going to, or returning from legislative sessions are not subject to civil process and are privileged from arrest except for felony or breach of the peace.

These are typical immunities granted to legislators in the federal and state constitutions. They operate only while the legislature is in session. The immunities are considered necessary to protect the public's interest in having legislators freely express themselves without fear of retribution, and devote themselves to state business without the trouble, worry, inconvenience, or harassment of court proceedings against them.

Section 7. Salary and Expenses

> Legislators shall receive annual salaries. They may receive a per diem allowance for expenses while in session and are entitled to travel expenses going to and from sessions. Presiding officers may receive additional compensation.

The question of legislators' salaries generated more debate at the consitutional convention than any other section under Article II. At issue was the way legislative pay might influence the composition of the legislature. Generally, the delegates favored sufficiently high pay to attract qualified, talented, and otherwise successful people to public office. There was opposition to substantial pay, however, on the grounds that office-holding should be largely a public-service contribution of citizens, and that high compensation might create a class of career legislators. In the end, the delegates adopted the concept of an annual salary (in contrast to per diem pay) but declined to establish in the constitution the amount of pay or a formula for calculating it (such as a percentage of the governor's salary). Thus, the legislature sets its own salary.

In 1981, legislators received annual salaries of $18,768. In addition, they received an expense allowance of $4,000 every year, and daily living allowance for each day of legislative session and each day of legislative committee work between sessions. (The basic rate is $67 but varies for legislators working in their home towns or in areas with higher-than-average costs of living.)

Section 8. Regular Sessions

> The legislature shall convene each year on the fourth Monday in January, but the month and day may be changed by law.

This section provides for annual legislative sessions. It is silent on the length of the sessions, which means that the legislature may continue to meet as long as it considers necessary. (About two-thirds of the state constitutions impose some restriction on the length of regular legislative sessions.) The framers of Alaska's constitution believed that the legislature should not be rushed in its deliberations, as the business of the state was too important to be transacted in hurried, infrequent sessions. While the delegates realized that good public policy does not necessarily result from abundant time for deliberation, they feared that ill-conceived and imprudent measures were more likely to result if there were constraints on the length and frequency of sessions.

Legislative sessions now regularly last over four months. Sessions of the first two legislatures (1959-1962) averaged 73 days; sessions of the last two (1977-1980) averaged 140 days. There is growing skepticism inside and outside the legislature that all of this time is spent wisely and productively. In 1978, the legislature asked Alaskans to cast an advisory vote on limiting the length of regular legislative sessions to 120 days. The proposition asked voters whether a constitutional amendment to that effect should be placed before the voters in the 1980 election. The voters overwhelmingly approved the proposition. This was only a gesture by the legislature, however, and a two-thirds majority has not been found to propose such an amendment to voters. On the question of session length, the past legislative viewpoint has been that the complexity and magnitude of public business has increased enormously since Alaska began receiving North Slope oil revenue, and that longer sessions are necessary to deal responsibly with this state business.

Section 9. Special Sessions

> Special sessions may be called by the governor or by vote of two-thirds of the legislators. The vote may be conducted by the legislative council or as prescribed by law. At special sessions called by the governor, legislation shall be limited to subjects designated in his proclamation calling the session, to subjects presented by him, and the reconsideration of bills vetoed by him after adjournment of the last regular session. Special sessions are limited to thirty days.

The language in the third sentence ("and the reconsideration of bills vetoed by him after adjournment of the last regular session") was added in 1976 by amendment. The legislature sought this amendment to expand its opportunity to override the governor's vetoes, and perhaps to discourage the governor from calling special sessions as well. (See also Section 16.) Allowance for special sessions under some conditions are common in all constitutions in order to permit the legislature to deal with emergencies. In the first 20 years of statehood, the legislature has met in special session seven times (the average length of these sessions was seven days: four of the sessions were three days). All of these sessions were called by the governor.

During special sessions called by the governor, the legislature may consider only those items that he designates. In dealing with these items, however, and in dealing with the items it chooses to in a special session called on its own motion, the legislature has power that is as broad as it is during a regular session.

Section 10. Adjournment

> Neither house may adjourn or recess for longer than three days unless the other concurs. If the two houses cannot agree on the time of adjournment and either house certifies the disagreement to the governor, he may adjourn the legislature.

The first sentence prevents one house from halting legislative business by unilaterally adjourning. The second sentence prevents the two houses from becoming deadlocked over the matter of adjournment. Thus, neither house can keep the legislature in session if the other house *and* the governor want the legislature to adjourn.

The mechanism for certifying disagreement to the governor has never been used, and there is no prescribed procedure for using it. There has been disagreement between the two houses over adjournment, however. Occasionally one house will simply adjourn out from under the other. So far, a constitutional crisis has been avoided by the house reconvening within three days or the other house adjourning within three days.

Section 11. Interim Committees

> There shall be a legislative council, and the legislature may establish other interim committees. The council and other interim committees may meet between legislative sessions. They may perform duties and employ personnel as provided by the legislature. Their members may receive an allowance for expenses while performing their duties.

The legislature may conduct legislative business between sessions and hire committee staff. These powers are essential for a strong and effective legislative body. Creation of the legislative council—a permanent committee of legislators—is mandated by this section. The council is presently composed of seven members from each chamber. It oversees the work of the Legislative Affairs Agency, which performs day-to-day administrative functions for the legislature such as hiring staff, printing bills, maintaining a reference library, and so on.

The second sentence of this section allows interim committees to meet between sessions. A result of this language, perhaps unintended by its authors, is that the main standing committees of the legislature (resources, state affairs, etc.) cannot function between sessions. When necessary, these have been reconstituted as interim committees to conform with the constitution.

A major political controversy over budgetary matters has developed in recent years between the legislative and executive branches, the solution to which has been sought in amendments to this section. The controversy, which has also developed in other states, concerns the ability of an interim committee of the legislature to exercise veto power over budget revisions by the governor when the legislature is not in session. While the legislature has asserted its authority to oversee budget revisions in the period between sessions, the executive has resisted on the grounds that such an arrangement violates the constitutional principle of separation of powers, and that it involves an unconstitutional delegation of legislative power to a committee. The courts sided with the executive, and in response, the legislature placed before the voters in 1980 a proposed constitutional amendment that would explicitly authorize the practice. The amendment was defeated.

Section 12. Rules

> The houses of each legislature shall adopt uniform rules of procedure. Each house may choose its officers and employees. Each is the judge of the election and qualifications of its members and may expel a member with the concurrence of two-thirds of its members.

> Each shall keep a journal of its proceedings. A majority of the membership of each house constitutes a quorum to do business, but a smaller number may adjourn from day to day and may compel attendance of absent members. The legislature shall regulate lobbying.

The several provisions of this section deal with matters of legislative procedures that are commonly found in constitutions.

All legislative bodies have rules of procedure to give order to the conduct of business and protect the rights of minority factions. Rules establish the priority and manner of consideration of questions, and they assure members of adequate notice of meeting and an opportunity to participate. Every governmental body has an inherent right to regulate its own procedure, subject to constitutional provision. This section of Alaska's constitution requires that both legislative chambers operate under a single set of rules. These are adopted at a joint meeting early in the opening session of each legislature.

The second and third sentences are traditional legislative prerogatives. In Alaska, the legislature has set procedures for contesting elections in the courts, but its constitutional authority to seat or expel members remains undiminished. On March 2, 1982, the Senate expelled a member who had been convicted of attempting to bribe another legislator. This is the only instance of a legislator being expelled in Alaska.

The journals kept by the House and Senate are official records of actions taken during each day of the session. They are not verbatim reports of discussion and debate.

A quorum is the minimum number of members required to be present before a legislative chamber can conduct official business. A quorum has the unquestioned right to compel the attendance of absent members (a call of the house), and this section gives that right to less than a quorum. ("The absence of the power of a legislative body to compel the attendance of all members at all times would destroy its ability to function as a legislative body"—Mason's Legislative Manual.)

The mandate to regulate lobbying reflects the convention's strong distrust of special interests. A.S. 24.45 complies with this directive by requiring lobbyists to register and disclose their incomes and expenditures for lobbying.

Section 13. Form of Bills

> Every bill shall be confined to one subject unless it is an appropriation bill or one codifying, revising, or rearranging existing laws. Bills for appropriations shall be confined to appropriations. The subject of each bill shall be expressed in the title. The enacting clause shall be: "Be it enacted by the Legislature of the State of Alaska."

The first sentence of this section is a familiar constitutional directive known as the "one subject" rule. It is intended to prevent, in the words of the state supreme court, "the inclusion of incongruous and unrelated matters in the same bill to get support for it which the several subjects might not separately command, and to guard against inadvertence, stealth and fraud in legislation" (Suber v. Alaska State Bond Commission, 414 P.2d 546; 1976). The courts have always construed this rule broadly, giving wide discretion to the legislature to decide what constitutes one subject.

Section 14. Passage of Bills
> The legislature shall establish the procedure for enactment of bills into law. No bill may become law unless it has passed three readings in each house on three separate days, except that any bill may be advanced from second to third reading on the same day by concurrence of three-fourths of the house considering it. No bill may become law without an affirmative vote of a majority of the membership of each house. The yeas and nays on final passage shall be entered in the journal.

These and formalities required by Section 13 give ordered procedure to the enactment of bills. The three-reading rule helps assure that bills will receive deliberation and that the legislature will know what it is voting on. (Amendments made to the text of a bill at the second or third reading are valid even though the amended bill is not read thereafter three times on three days.) The last sentence of this section assures that the required majority has voted to pass a bill, and that there is a public record of the vote cast by each legislator.

A bill is a proposed law. A resolution is an expression of the will of the legislative chamber that enacts it. It does not become a law, and therefore is not required by the constitution to follow the procedures of this and other sections dealing with the enactment of laws. There has been dispute between the legislative and executive branches over the use of joint resolutions of the legislature to annul administrative regulations. This dispute found its way to court, where the legislature lost. The supreme court said that acts of the legislature which bind others outside the legislature must take the form of a bill and follow the procedures of a bill as required by this section and Section 13, and that they must be subject to the governor's veto (State v. ALIVE Voluntary, 606 P.2d 769; 1980). In response to this setback in court, the legislature put before the voters in 1980 a constitutional amendment that would permit the annulment of regulations by joint resolution, but it failed to be ratified.

Section 15. Veto
> The governor may veto bills passed by the legislature. He may, by veto, strike or reduce items in appropriation bills. He shall return any vetoed bill, with a statement of his objections, to the house of origin.

The veto power is a central feature of the system of checks and balances in American constitutional government, and it is intended to prevent ill-conceived legislation from becoming law. The governor may veto bills for any reason, and does so usually because of objection to them as a matter of public policy or because of possible constitutional defects. By this provision, the governor can exercise the veto only over an entire bill, not over individual parts of it, except for appropriation bills. The power of Alaska's governor to veto "line items" in appropriation bills is exceptional among the states, and it greatly enhances the governor's power.

Section 16. Action Upon Veto
> Upon receipt of a veto message during a regular session of the legislature, the legislature shall meet immediately in joint session and reconsider passage of the vetoed bill or item. Bills to raise revenue and appropriation bills or items, although vetoed, become law by affirmative vote of three-fourths of the membership of the legislature. Other vetoed bills become law by affirmative vote of two-thirds of the membership of the legislature. Bills vetoed after adjournment of the first regular session of the legislature shall be reconsidered by the legislature sitting as one body no later than the fifth day of the next regular or special session of that legislature. Bills vetoed after adjournment of the second regular session shall be reconsidered by the legislature sitting as one body no later than the fifth day of a special session of that legislature, if one is called. The vote on reconsideration of a vetoed bill shall be entered on the journals of both houses.

This section was amended in 1976 by inserting the words "during a regular session of the legislature" in the first sentence and adding the fourth and fifth sentences. The amendment was sought by the legislature to enhance its ability to reconsider vetoed bills. A large number of bills are typically passed at the very end of a session, and the legislature has adjourned when the governor's veto power is exercised. Prior to this amendment, the legislature would have to call itself into a special session to reconsider a vetoed item (it has actually never done so). It may still have to resort to a special session if the veto occurs after the end of a second regular session, but it can now reconsider in the early days of the second session bills vetoed after the end of the first session.

The requirement in this section that the legislature vote as one body is unusual among the states. Its effect is to make it easier to override a veto than if a two-thirds majority were required in each house. (Note that the requirement for a vote of two-thirds majority in each house allows one-third of one house—seven senators, for example—to frustrate majorities in both houses. Thus, the constitution only rarely requires a special majority in each house.) Also unusual is the requirement for three-fourths of the legislature to vote to override the veto of an appropriation or new revenue bill. It makes the override particularly difficult.

Section 17. Bills Not Signed

A bill becomes law if, while the legislature is in session, the governor neither signs nor vetoes it within fifteen days, Sundays excepted, after its delivery to him. If the legislature is not in session and the governor neither signs nor vetoes a bill within twenty days, Sundays excepted, after its delivery to him, the bill becomes law.

According to the terms of this section, bills can become law without the governor's signature. In many other constitutional schemes, a bill fails to become law without the governor's signature. By this section, our constitution allows no such "pocket veto." (Remember that Section 15 requires an explanation of every veto by the governor.)

Section 18. Effective Date

Laws passed by the legislature become effective ninety days after enactment. The legislature may, by concurrence of two-thirds of the membership of each house, provide for another effective date.

Unless it is set otherwise by a separate vote of two-thirds of the legislature, the effective date of a law is 90 days after it is passed. Frequently, the legislature does provide for an immediate effective date of its acts. The 90-day interval between enactment and effect of a law is intended to provide a fair opportunity to those people affected by the legislation to learn of the law they must live by and to prepare for the new situation.

Section 19. Local or Special Acts

The legislature shall pass no local or special act if a general act can be made applicable. Whether a general act can be made applicable shall be subject to judicial determination. Local acts necessitating appropriations by a political subdivision may not become effective unless approved by a majority of the qualified voters voting thereon in the subdivision affected.

Here is a safeguard against laws that selectively benefit or discriminate against a particular community or particular people. A hypothetical example of the former would be a law that prohibits Fairbanks from expanding its boundaries; a hypothetical example of the latter would be an act granting a divorce to John and Jane Doe. The constitutional guarantee against legislative intrusion in local affairs is essential for effective home rule (see Article X, Sections 9-11). The courts have held that the prohibition against local acts does not invalidate laws that operate only on limited geographical areas if the laws are reasonably related to a matter of statewide concern or common interest (for example, the location of the state capital). In cases where no statewide or common interest is involved, a law is invalid under this section if a general law is possible. Thus in 1975, the court struck down an act of the legislature which established a special set of procedures for the formation of the proposed Eagle River-Chugiak Borough in the Anchorage area (Abrams v. State, 534 P.2d; 1975).

There have been no court cases involving an alleged violation of the prohibition against "special" acts, nor has the legislature passed a law of the type referred to in the third sentence of this section.

Section 20. Impeachment

> All civil officers of the State are subject to impeachment by the legislature. Impeachment shall originate in the senate and must be approved by a two-thirds vote of its members. The motion for impeachment shall list fully the basis for the proceeding. Trial on impeachment shall be conducted by the house of representatives. A supreme court justice designated by the court shall preside at the trial. Concurrence of two-thirds of the members of the house is required for a judgment of impeachment. The judgment may not extend beyond removal from office, but shall not prevent proceedings in the courts on the same or related charges.

For some reason, the convention delegates reversed the federal impeachment procedure, which is impeachment by the House and trial by the Senate.

Section 21. Suits Against The State

> The legislature shall establish procedures for suits against the State.

The long-established principle of sovereign immunity, that a state cannot be sued without its permission, is modified in Alaska by this constitutional provision. It commands the legislature to provide general procedures for suits against the state so that justice for citizens may be served.

Article III
The Executive

Article III creates the executive branch of government and vests the governor with the executive power of the state. The constitutional convention delegates created a strong governor for the same reason they created a strong legislature: they believed that effective and responsible state government required that each branch have broad and uncomplicated powers to carry out its respective duties.

Few state constitutions grant as much authority to the governor as does Alaska's. This is because most of the other constitutions were written with a history of tyrannical or corrupt executives in mind. Alaska's experience was different. Here, the historical problems with executive authority were its weakness and ineffectiveness. Territorial governors shared executive power with federal bureaucracies, with boards and commissions created by the territorial legislature, and with elected department heads. Frustration with this weak executive power in the territorial government was largely responsible for Alaska's constitutional provisions for a strong governor. (Also, the constitutional reform movement favored a strong executive, and the model constitution of the National Municipal League creates a powerful governor.)

The primary source of the governor's power in Alaska is Article III. Sections 22-25 are especially important. They create a centralized administrative structure that is directly accountable to the governor. Additional grants of executive power are found in other articles of the constitution, such as Article II, which grants the veto power, and Article IX, which gives the authority to prepare an executive budget.

Section 1. Executive Power
The executive power of the State is vested in the governor.

This section and Section 16 directly grant to the governor the executive power of the state.

Section 2. Governor: Qualifications
> The governor shall be at least thirty years of age and a qualified voter of the State. He shall have been a resident of Alaska at least seven years immediately preceding his filing for office, and he shall have been a citizen of the United States for at least seven years.

These qualifications are typical of state constitutional provisions generally. They differ from the U.S. constitutional qualifications for president, who must be at least 35, a natural-born citizen, and a resident for 14 years.

Section 3. Election
> The governor shall be chosen by the qualified voters of the State at a general election. The candidate receiving the greatest number of votes shall be governor.

This provision, too, is typical of state constitutions. A plurality of votes rather than a majority vote is required to elect the governor. Thus, there is no runoff election among two top candidates after a general election with several candidates. In the 1980 general election, for example, there were five candidates—two from the major parties, two from minor parties, and one write-in. The winner, Jay Hammond, received about 38 percent of the vote.

Section 4. Term of Office
> The term of office of the governor is four years, beginning at noon on the first Monday in December following his election and ending at noon on the first Monday in December four years later.

Most of the states have a four-year term for governor. Only four states have a two-year term. A measure often discussed but not yet adopted anywhere is a single six-year term for governor. This is thought to be beneficial because it would eliminate the political pressures associated with running for reelection. However, it would also reduce the public accountability of the governor's office.

Alaska's constitution sets the beginning of the governor's term early in December so that an incoming governor has time to begin preparation of the budget before the legislature convenes in January. Alaska is one of few states with a December date for the beginning of the governor's term.

Section 5. Limit on Tenure
> No person who has been elected governor for two full successive

> terms shall be again eligible to hold that office until one full term has intervened.

This constitutional prohibition against serving more than two successive terms in office is intended to prevent the accumulation of excessive power by the governor and administrative officials.

Section 6. Dual Office Holding

> The governor shall not hold any other office or position of profit under the United States, the State, or its political subdivisions.

This provision, like that pertaining to legislators, is intended to prevent conflicts of interest and the accumulation of excessive power.

Section 7. Lieutenant Governor: Duties

> There shall be a lieutenant governor. He shall have the same qualifications as the governor and serve for the same term. He shall perform such duties as may be prescribed by law and as may be delegated to him by the governor.

An amendment to the constitution in 1970 changed the title of this office from secretary of state to lieutenant governor, presumably because the new title carried more prestige. Whether or not to create an office of lieutenant governor at all was seriously debated by the delegates at the constitutional convention. In the end they decided it was desirable to have an elected successor to the governor. They wanted a working successor, but left it to the legislature and the governor to define the scope of his or her duties. However, elsewhere in the constitution (Articles XI and XIII) specific electoral duties are assigned to the lieutenant governor, a traditional responsibility of this office. The legislature has expanded these few specific constitutional duties by making the lieutenant governor the overseer of elections generally. Beyond that, however, the position carries no significant statutory duties, and the role of the lieutenant governor in the affairs of the state is largely limited to whatever executive duties the governor grants to the person holding the office.

Section 8. Election

> The lieutenant governor shall be nominated in the manner provided by law for nominating candidates for other elective offices. In the general election the votes cast for a candidate for governor shall be considered as cast also for the candidate for lieutenant governor running jointly with him. The candidate whose name appears on the ballot jointly with that of the successful candidate for governor shall be elected lieutenant governor.

The convention delegates wanted the lieutenant governor to be popularly elected in the event he or she should suddenly accede to the office of governor. They also wanted the lieutenant governor to be compatible with the governor, at least in the matter of political party membership. Therefore they provided that candidates would stand independently in the primary election, and the winner in each party would be paired with that party's gubernatorial nominee in the general election. Thus, in Alaska the governor and lieutenant governor are elected together. In contrast, about one-half the states elect the lieutenant governor independently in the general election, which creates the possibility of this person being of a different political party.

Section 9. Acting Governor

> In case of the temporary absence of the governor from office, the lieutenant governor shall serve as acting governor.

This is a conventional function of the lieutenant governor.

Section 10. Succession: Failure to Qualify

> If the governor-elect dies, resigns, or is disqualified, the lieutenant governor elected with him shall succeed to the office of governor for the full term. If the governor-elect fails to assume office for any other reason, the lieutenant governor elected with him shall serve as acting governor, and shall succeed to the office if the governor-elect does not assume his office within six months of the beginning of the term.

Section 11. Vacancy

> In case of a vacancy in the office of governor for any reason, the lieutenant governor shall succeed to the office for the remainder of the term.

These two sections specify the succession to the office of the governor by the lieutenant governor in the event a vacancy occurs. One section deals with a governor-elect and the other with a governor in office, but the result of succession is the same. These and subsequent provisions on succession were carefully developed by the convention to cover contingencies overlooked by other constitutions.

Section 12. Absence

> Whenever for a period of six months, a governor has been continuously absent from office or has been unable to discharge the duties of his office by reason of mental or physical disability, the office shall be deemed vacant. The procedure for determining absence and disability shall be prescribed by law.

The legislature has not established a procedure for determining absence and disability within the meaning of this section. This is unfortunate, because it might be difficult to specify these procedures quickly in case the need for them arose.

Section 13. Further Succession

> Provision shall be made by law for succession to the office of governor and for an acting governor in the event that the lieutenant governor is unable to succeed to the office or act as governor. No election of a lieutenant governor shall be held except at the time of electing a governor.

The legislature has provided, pursuant to this section, that after taking office, the governor is to appoint a successor to the lieutenant governor ("from among the officers who head principal departments of the state government or otherwise"), who must be confirmed by a majority of the legislature meeting in joint session. In the event a vacancy occurs in the office of lieutenant governor, the person would assume the position. However, this appointed person could never succeed to the office of governor. He or she could serve only as acting governor until a special election is held to elect a new governor and lieutenant governor. (See A.S. 44.19.040.)

Section 14. Title and Authority

> When the lieutenant governor succeeds to the office of governor, he shall have the title, powers, duties, and emoluments of that office.

This is a standard constitutional provision.

Section 15. Compensation

> The compensation of the governor and the lieutenant governor shall be prescribed by law and shall not be diminished during their term of office, unless by general law applying to all salaried officers of the State.

The legislature may not drive the governor from office by reducing his or her salary. A similar provision protects judges. (Article IV, Section 13.) This protection is a safeguard of the separation of powers. An across-the-board salary reduction would presumably not be made as a punitive action against select people.

Section 16. Governor: Authority

> The governor shall be responsible for the faithful execution of the laws. He may, by appropriate court action or proceeding brought in the name of the State, enforce compliance with any constitutional or legislative mandate, or restrain violation of any constitutional or legislative power, duty, or right by any officer, department, or

> agency of the State or any of its political subdivisions. This authority shall not be construed to authorize any action or proceeding against the legislature.

This language was adopted by the convention delegates from the model constitution of the National Municipal League. Only New Jersey has a similar provision. By its terms, the governor may intervene in or initiate lawsuits on behalf of the state or individuals, even when the state does not otherwise have standing in the case, if necessary to ensure "the faithful execution of the laws." The last sentence protects the integrity of the separation of powers by prohibiting the governor from suing the legislature.

Section 17. Convening Legislature

> Whenever the governor considers it in the public interest, he may convene the legislature, either house, or the two houses in joint session.

Authority to convene the legislature is a potentially important source of gubernatorial power. How effective the governor is in utilizing this power depends on many factors. In certain circumstances it may be used to influence a recalcitrant legislature. For example, the first session of the Twelfth Legislature adjourned without passing a constitutional amendment to limit state spending, a legislative priority of the governor. He therefore called a special session to deal with the subject, and the legislature adopted an amendment to go before the voters for ratification in 1982.

By this section, the governor can call either or both houses into session. The reason a governor might call only one house into session is to complete action on a bill already passed by the other house.

Section 18. Message to Legislature

> The governor shall, at the beginning of each session, and may at other times, give the legislature information concerning the affairs of the State and recommend the measures he considers necessary.

While this power may not seem important on its face, it enhances the governor's authority because it gives the governor the ability to raise public policy issues and initiate debate and consideration of them. The governor's message may help set the agenda of the legislature.

Section 19. Military Authority

> The governor is commander-in-chief of the armed forces of the State. He may call out these forces to execute the laws, suppress or prevent insurrection or lawless violence, or repel invasion. The gover-

nor, as provided by law, shall appoint all general and flag officers of the armed forces of the State, subject to confirmation by a majority of the members of the legislature in joint session. He shall appoint and commission all other officers.

These are traditional grants of constitutional power to the office of the governor. Armed forces of the state are the members of the Alaska National Guard.

Section 20. Martial Law

The governor may proclaim martial law when the public safety requires it in case of rebellion or actual or imminent invasion. Martial law shall not continue for longer than twenty days without the approval of a majority of the members of the legislature in joint session.

Under martial law, normal civil liberties may be suspended. The governor may impose martial law in the face of rebellion or invasion, but the legislature must confirm the urgency of the situation after 20 days.

Section 21. Executive Clemency

Subject to procedure prescribed by law, the governor may grant pardons, commutations, and reprieves, and may suspend and remit fines and forfeitures. This power shall not extend to impeachment. A parole system shall be provided by law.

Granting pardons and reprieves is a traditional executive function. However, the phrase, "subject to procedure prescribed by law," provides an opportunity for the legislature to prevent political abuses of the clemency power and mistakes of judgment about such things as the psychological fitness of a prisoner for release. However, the legislature has not yet prescribed procedures for executive grants of clemency under this section.

Section 22. Executive Branch

All executive and administrative offices, departments, and agencies of the state government and their respective functions, powers, and duties shall be allocated by law among and within not more than twenty principal departments, so as to group them as far as practicable according to major purposes. Regulatory, quasi-judicial, and temporary agencies may be established by law and need not be allocated within a principal department.

Limiting the number of executive departments to twenty expresses the constitutional objective of keeping the executive branch streamlined, efficient, and easily managed. It reflects the modern concept of effective organizational structure. Alaska presently has fifteen principal departments (including the office of the governor), and has never had more than seventeen.

Section 23. Reorganization

> The governor may make changes in the organization of the executive branch or in the assignment of functions among its units which he considers necessary for efficient administration. Where these changes require the force of law, they shall be set forth in executive orders. The legislature shall have sixty days of a regular session, or a full session if of shorter duration, to disapprove these executive orders. Unless disapproved by resolution concurred in by a majority of the members in joint session, these orders become effective at a date thereafter to be designated by the governor.

This section is unusual among state constitutions. It gives to the governor the initiative for administrative reorganization. The legislature normally prescribes by law the functions and structure of the principal executive departments and administrative agencies of state government. Under this section, however, the governor can reorganize these departments and agencies. The legislature may disapprove the reorganization (by a majority of both houses meeting in joint session) within sixty days of the governor's executive order. This is considered one of the major features of Alaska's "strong governor" constitutional scheme.

Section 24. Supervision

> Each principal department shall be under the supervision of the governor.

Section 25. Department Heads

> The head of each principal department shall be a single executive unless otherwise provided by law. He shall be appointed by the governor, subject to confirmation by a majority of the members of the legislature in joint session, and shall serve at the pleasure of the governor, except as otherwise provided in this article with respect to the lieutenant governor. The heads of all principal departments shall be citizens of the United States.

In many other states, two, three, four, or more department heads may be elected, which means that the activities of these departments and the realm of public policy they encompass are beyond the direct control of the governor. Alaska's constitution prevents this diffusion of executive authority. It specifies that each department is supervised by the governor, and it gives the governor a means to make the supervision effective, namely the power to appoint and remove department heads.

While there was general agreement among the convention delegates that Alaska should have a centralized and accountable system of executive administration, they bowed to the political power of two interest groups at the convention, education and fish and game. Both feared that the governor might not be sufficiently responsive to their concerns and that a board composed of members from their own ranks would provide much more reliable departmental leadership. (They expressed this fear at the convention with the argument that educational policy and fish and game management might be caught up in "politics" if the governor were allowed to appoint department heads in these areas.) After long and acrimonious debate about how to structure these boards, the delegates agreed upon the present language ("the head of each principal department shall be a single executive unless otherwise provided by law") which allowed the legislature to resolve the matter.

Immediately after statehood the legislature established boards at the head of the departments of education and fish and game (the latter now has two boards). In the early years of statehood, there was discussion of placing a board at the head of the highway department, but it came to nothing. In recent years, there has been no further serious consideration of putting boards in charge of executive departments.

A proposal is frequently advanced to amend the constitution to provide for an elected attorney general. (About forty states require the election of the attorney general.) Since the attorney general advises the governor on legal matters, it is thought by some that his (or her) political independence from the governor would result in a more objective legal perspective. An assessment of the merits of this proposal is well beyond the scope of this discussion, but it should be noted that such a change would be a further retreat from the original constitutional objective of a centralized and accountable executive administration.

A notable constitutional law case developed over interpretation of language in this section and Section 26 which gives the legislature authority to confirm the governor's appointments of heads of major departments. Confirmation authority of this type is a traditional legislative "check and balance" on the executive branch. The Alaska legislature asserted that it could by law extend its authority to confirm appointments to deputy department heads as well as department heads, on the ground that these positions involve substantial policy-making authority. The governor refused to submit names of his department deputy heads to the legislature, which sued. The supreme court ruled against the legislature (Bradner v. Hammond,

553 P.2d1; 1976). It said that the power to confirm did not extend beyond the express limits of the constitution and that the legislature's action violated the principle of separation of powers. Thus rebuffed, the legislature in 1980 placed a proposed constitutional amendment before the voters that would give the legislature explicit authority to determine which executive appointees would be subject to confirmation. The amendment failed to be ratified by the voters.

Section 26. Boards and Commissions

> When a board or commission is at the head of a principal department or a regulatory or quasi-judicial agency, its members shall be appointed by the governor, subject to confirmation by a majority of the members of the legislature in joint session, and may be removed as provided by law. They shall be citizens of the United States. The board or commission may appoint a principal executive officer when authorized by law, but the appointment shall be subject to the approval of the governor.

Members of boards and commissions are appointed by the governor and confirmed by the legislature. Thus, even though there is a policy-making board at the head of an executive department, the governor retains the power to appoint the members of the board and to veto a board's choice of its principal executive officer. However, the constitution permits the legislature to determine how these board members are removed. The statutes governing the respective boards and commissions specify the terms of removal. In the case of the state board of education, for example, the law provides that the members serve at the pleasure of the governor. In the case of the boards of fisheries and game, however, the law restricts the governor's power of removal to cases of "inefficiency, neglect of duty, or misconduct in office."

The use of joint sessions to confirm appointments is unusual. The more traditional method is to require action by one house only, or by both houses voting separately.

Section 27. Recess Appointments

> The governor may make appointments to fill vacancies occurring during a recess of the legislature, in offices requiring confirmation by the legislature. The duration of such appointments shall be prescribed by law.

This section is intended to ensure that a department does not go without a head (commissioner) during the interval between legislative sessions. A set of general procedures for legislative confirmation has been established by the legislature as authorized by this section (see A.S. 39.05.080).

Article IV
The Judiciary

Like Alaska's constitution as a whole, the judiciary article is widely regarded as a good example of constitutional workmanship. It creates a strong and effective third branch of government. These attributes of the judicial system derive from its efficiency, its independence, and the method of its accountability to the people.

Alaska's court system is efficient when compared to most others because it is unified. This means that all of the courts are part of a single state system; they are administered from one place; they all operate under the same rules; and they are all financed by the state legislature. We recognize this type of organization in the federal courts. In many states, however, the court system is fragmented: there may be municipal courts, courts of special jurisdictions, county courts, and state appellate courts—each with its own peculiar jurisdiction, its own rules and procedures, its own administration, and source of finance. Court reforms long sought in these older states are embodied in Alaska's constitution.

The independence of Alaska's courts is protected by various means. Most important is the method of selecting judges. Article IV requires that judges be appointed by the governor from a list of nominees submitted by an independent body, the judicial council, described in Section 8 below. Thus, judgeships are not among the spoils of office. Also, judges are not elected; the constitutional convention delegates had little confidence in elections producing qualified judges. Appointed judges do not need to worry about how their decisions will affect their immediate chances of reelection. Nor do they need to finance expensive campaigns from donations by private interests.

Accountability of appointed judges to the people is provided by periodic votes of confidence in which judges stand before the electorate on their own records, without party labels. The question before the voters is simply whether the judges should remain in office. These "retention elections" occur three years after a judge is appointed and at six- or ten-year intervals thereafter. A judge can be impeached by the legislature or removed from the bench if incapacitated, but not recalled by the voters. Article IV seems to have worked well in the first twenty years of statehood. Four amendments have been made, but they do not make basic changes in the system. Although there is recurrent criticism of aspects of Alaska's judiciary article, such as the retention election, these concerns have not resulted in proposed constitutional amendments being placed before the voters for ratification.

Section 1. Judicial Power and Jurisdiction

> The judicial power of the State is vested in a supreme court, a superior court and the courts established by the legislature. The jurisdiction of courts shall be prescribed by law. The courts shall constitute a unified judicial system for operation and administration. Judicial districts shall be established by law.

This section vests the judicial power of the state in the unified court system which, at a minimum, is composed of a supreme court and a superior court. The legislature has elaborated on this basic court system under the authority granted by this section. It has created two additional courts: a district court and an appellate court. The full jurisdiction of these non-constitutional courts as well as the supreme court and the superior court are described in Title 22 of the Alaska Statutes.

Section 2. Supreme Court

> (a) The supreme court shall be the highest court of the State, with final appellate jurisdiction. It shall consist of three justices, one of whom is chief justice. The number of justices may be increased by law upon the request of the supreme court.
>
> (b) The chief justice shall be selected from among the justices of the supreme court by a majority vote of the justices. His term of office as chief justice is three years. A justice may serve more than one term as chief justice but he may not serve consecutive terms in that office.

This section was amended in 1970 by adding paragraph (b). Prior to the amendment, the constitution was silent on how the chief justice was to be selected, and it was the practice for the governor to make the designation. In the late 1960s, there was a great deal of conflict between the chief justice and the state bar association and within the court system itself over administrative policies and decisions of the chief justice. That situation gave rise to the amendment. It prevents the accumulation of too much power in one justice and eliminates the role of the governor in designating the chief justice.

At the present time there are five supreme court justices.

Section 3. Superior Court
> The superior court shall be the trial court of general jurisdiction and shall consist of five judges. The number of judges may be changed by law.

The superior court is the constitutional court with general jurisdiction over all civil and criminal matters. Its general jurisdiction is now shared, however, with the district court—which, according to statute, handles cases that involve less money or less severe punishments than those that are heard by the superior court. There are currently 23 superior court judges distributed among four judicial districts in Alaska, and 16 district court judges (there are also 62 magistrates in the district court).

Section 4. Qualifications of Justices and Judges
> Supreme court justices and superior court judges shall be citizens of the United States and of the State, licensed to practice law in the State, and possessing any additional qualifications prescribed by law. Judges of other courts shall be selected in a manner, for terms, and with qualifications prescribed by law.

The legislature has required that, in addition to meeting these minimum qualifications, supreme court justices and superior court judges must have been residents of the state for three years immediately preceding their appointment, and engaged in the active practice of law for eight and five years respectively prior to their appointment. Appellate and district court judges must meet the same basic qualifications and must have been in the active practice of law for eight and three years respectively.

Section 5. Nomination and Appointment
> The governor shall fill any vacancy in an office of supreme court justice or superior court judge by appointing one of two or more persons nominated by the judicial council.

Judges are appointed by the governor from a list of at least two names submitted to him by the judicial council. (See Section 8 below.) The legislature has no role in the selection or confirmation of judges.

Section 6. Approval or Rejection

Each supreme court justice and superior court judge shall, in the manner provided by law, be subject to approval or rejection on a nonpartisan ballot at the first general election held more than three years after his appointment. Thereafter, each supreme court justice shall be subject to approval or rejection in a like manner every tenth year, and each superior court judge, every sixth year.

The voters may remove a judge they believe is unfit for office. However, the procedure does not allow them to sweep away a judge on a popular whim or impulse, and it gives a new judge time to prove himself. Thus, it is designed to balance the need for judicial independence with the need for public accountability.

Despite the theoretical appeal of retention elections, some people question their effectiveness in practice. They claim that voters do not seem to be well enough informed about the performance of individual judges to make critical choices about their retention. In Alaska every judge but one who has faced the electorate has been retained in office, and the defeated judge was one widely respected by his peers. (There have been about 100 retention elections in the first 20 years of statehood.) The form of the retention election biases the outcome in favor of a yes vote (there is no opposition to the judge standing for reelection; the judge is nonpartisan and has the advantage of already being in office). Doubts about the system have grown stronger since 1975, when the legislature required the judicial council to begin evaluating judges who are standing for reelection and to publish the results prior to the election. Several judges have been declared unqualified for office as a result of this evaluation, but the voters have retained them anyway.

Section 7. Vacancy

The office of any supreme court justice or superior court judge becomes vacant ninety days after the election at which he is rejected by a majority of those voting on the question, or for which he fails to file his declaration of candidacy to succeed himself.

These procedures implement Section 6.

Section 8. Judicial Council

The judicial council shall consist of seven members. Three attorney members shall be appointed for six-year terms by the governing body of the organized state bar. Three non-attorney members shall be appointed for six-year terms by the governor subject to confirmation by a majority of the members of the legislature in joint session. Vacancies shall be filled for the unexpired term in like manner. Appointments shall be made with due consideration to area repre-

> sentation and without regard to political affiliation. The chief justice of the supreme court shall be ex officio the seventh member and chairman of the judicial council. No member of the judicial council, except the chief justice, may hold any other office or position of profit under the United States or the State. The judicial council shall act by concurrence of four or more members and according to rules which it adopts.

Note that four members of the judicial council must be lawyers and three must be laymen. Note also that three of the lawyers are appointed by the Alaska Bar Association, a private professional association. The governor appoints the lay members. The seventh member is the chief justice of the supreme court. This constitutional scheme was drawn up by a committee of the constitutional convention composed largely of lawyers. It has been criticized for giving too much influence to a private professional society in the selection of Alaska's judiciary. However serious this shortcoming of the section, and however controversial some appointments to the council by the bar association may have been, the judicial council has not yet been criticized for producing poor nominees for appointment to the bench.

Section 9. Additional Duties

> The judicial council shall conduct studies for improvement of the administration of justice, and make reports and recommendations to the supreme court and to the legislature at intervals of not more than two years. The judicial council shall perform other duties assigned by law.

The primary constitutional duty of the judicial council is to submit names of candidates for judicial appointment to the governor (Section 5). This section gives it the additional duty of studying the judicial system and recommending improvements. Thus, for example, the judicial council has studied such matters as plea bargaining, sentencing, and the use of the grand jury. The legislature has not added substantially to the duties of the council.

Section 10. Commission on Judicial Qualifications

> The commission on judicial qualifications shall consist of nine members, as follows: one justice of the supreme court, elected by the justices of the supreme court; three judges of the superior court, elected by the judges of the superior court; one judge of the district court, elected by the judges of the district court; two members who have practiced law in this state for ten years, appointed by the governing body of the organized bar; and two persons who are not judges, retired judges, or members of the state bar, appointed by the governor and subject to confirmation by a majority of the members

> of the legislature in joint session. In addition to being subject to impeachment under Section 12 of this article, a justice or judge may be disqualified from acting as such and may be suspended, removed from office, retired, or censured by the supreme court upon the recommendation of the commission. The powers and duties of the commission and the bases for judicial disqualification shall be established by law.

This entire section, which was adopted by an amendment in 1968, replaced the original section. The original section specified a procedure for removing a judge for being incapacitated but not one for removing a judge for being unqualified. The new section creates a commission on judicial qualifications to make recommendations to the supreme court which the court may use to suspend, remove from office, retire, or censure a judge. The provisions of this section were based on the new judiciary article of California's constitution.

Section 11. Retirement

> Justices and judges shall be retired at the age of seventy except as provided in this article. The basis and amount of retirement pay shall be prescribed by law. Retired judges shall render no further service on the bench except for special assignments as provided by court rule.

Framers of the constitution believed that mandatory retirement of judges at age seventy was necessary to prevent the possibility that a person of failing intellectual powers might remain on the bench.

Section 12. Impeachment

> Impeachment of any justice or judge for malfeasance or misfeasance in the performance of his official duties shall be according to procedure prescribed for civil officers.

Judges in Alaska are not exempt from impeachment (although they are exempt from recall). The impeachment procedure is described in Article II, Section 20.

Section 13. Compensation

> Justices, judges, and members of the judicial council and the commission on judicial qualifications shall receive compensation as prescribed by law. Compensation of justices and judges shall not be diminished during their terms of office, unless by general law applying to all salaried officers of the State.

The prohibition in this section against reducing the salaries of judges in office is a means of safeguarding the independence of the judiciary. This and identical protection for the governor and lieutenant governor in Article III, Section 15, helps protect the integrity of the three branches of government.

Section 14. Restrictions

> Supreme court justices and superior court judges while holding office may not practice law, hold office in a political party, or hold any other office or position of profit under the United States, the State, or its political subdivisions. Any supreme court justice or superior court judge filing for another elective public office forfeits his judicial position.

These restrictions on the activities of judges serve the same purposes as similar restrictions on dual office holding by legislators and the governor: to prevent conflicts of interest, concentration of power, and violations of the separation of powers. Presumably, this section would prevent a judge from being a delegate to the constitutional convention. This provision required a state judge to resign his position as a Regent of the University of Alaska.

Section 15. Rule-making Power

> The supreme court shall make and promulgate rules governing the administration of all courts. It shall make and promulgate rules governing practice and procedure in civil and criminal cases in all courts. These rules may be changed by the legislature by two-thirds vote of the members elected to each house.

The supreme court's power to make rules for all state courts is an important means of insuring unity and integration of the entire judicial system. As a check on the judicial branch, however, the constitution permits the legislature to oversee the supreme court's rules. The legislature does, on occasion, exercise its authority to change rules adopted by the court.

Section 16. Court Administration

> The chief justice of the supreme court shall be the administrative head of all courts. He may assign judges from one court or division thereof to another for temporary service. The chief justice shall, with the approval of the supreme court, appoint an administrative director to serve at the pleasure of the supreme court and to supervise the administrative operations of the judicial system.

This section further centralizes the operation of the court system in the supreme court. It was amended in 1970 to make the administrator of the court system responsible to the entire court rather than to the chief justice alone. This change sought to dilute the power of the chief justice; like the amendment of Section 2, it was an outgrowth of conflicts over the exercise of power by the first chief justice under the original constitutional provisions.

Article V
Suffrage and Elections

Article V deals with voting and elections.[3] The most important functions of Article V are to establish the qualifications for voting and to guarantee the right to vote by all who meet those qualifications. The first section, which establishes the qualifications to vote in Alaska, has been amended four times (more than any other section of the constitution). These amendments have liberalized the qualifications for voting by authorizing the legislature to modify residency requirements for voting in presidential elections; lowering the voting age from 19 to 18; eliminating a language requirement; and reducing residency requirements from one year to thirty days. These changes reflect a trend in federal court decisions that compel state governments to eliminate impediments to vote that discriminate against certain groups of people. (For example, residency requirements discriminate against people who exercise their right to move freely about the United States.)

The authors of Alaska's constitution believed that the legislature should establish the details of the election process so they could easily be changed when necessary. Thus, many important provisions for voting, electioneering, and conducting elections are found in the state's election code, Title 15 of the Alaska Statutes, rather than in the constitution.

Section 1. Qualified Voters

> Every citizen of the United States who is at least eighteen years of age, who meets registration residency requirements which may be prescribed by law, and who is qualified to vote under this article, may vote in any state or local election. A voter shall have been, immediately preceding the election, a thirty-day resident of the elec-

---

[3]Suffrage means the right to vote or the exercise of that right.

tion district in which he seeks to vote, except that for purposes of voting for President and Vice President of the United States other residency requirements may be prescribed by law. Additional voting qualifications may be prescribed by law for bond issue elections of political subdivisions.

As it originally appeared in the constitution, Section 1 read:

Every citizen of the United States who is at least nineteen years of age, who meets registration requirements which may be prescribed by law, and who is qualified to vote under this article, may vote in any state or local election. He shall have been, immediately preceding the election, for one year a resident of Alaska and for thirty days a resident of the election district in which he seeks to vote. He shall be able to read or speak the English language as prescribed by law, unless prevented by physical disability. Additional voting qualifications may be prescribed by law for bond issue elections of political subdivisions.

This language was first amended in 1966, when the clause "except that for purposes of voting for President and Vice President of the United States other residency requirements may be prescribed by law." A second amendment in 1970 lowered the voting age to 18 years. (A short time later the 26th Amendment to the U.S. Constitution set the voting age at 18 in all of the states, which supersedes state constitutional provisions.)

A third amendment to Section 1, also made in 1970, eliminated the requirement to read or speak English as a prerequisite to voting. A fourth amendment ratified in 1972 changed the durational residency requirement from 1 year to 30 days.

These changes (except the minimum voting age) were largely responses to U.S. Supreme Court decisions that found state voter qualifications to be too restrictive. For example, when the court overturned Tennessee's one-year residency requirement in Dunn v. Blumstein (405 U.S. 330; 1972), it became clear that Alaska's constitution would have to be changed.

At the present time, there is no residency requirement for voting in presidential elections (see A.S. 15.05.12 for voter qualifications in presidential elections).

Additional or different qualifications for voting in local bond issue elections are now unconstitutional. The U.S. Supreme Court has ruled that people who do not own property may not be excluded from voting on bond issues, even though the bonds are typically paid off by assessments on real estate.

Section 2. Disqualification

No person may vote who has been convicted of a felony involving moral turpitude unless his civil rights have been restored. No person may vote who has been judicially determined to be of unsound mind unless the disability has been removed.

Felonies involving moral turpitude are defined in the statutes as "those crimes which are immoral or wrong in themselves such as murder, sexual assault, robbery, kidnapping, incest, arson, burglary, theft and forgery." (A.S. 15.15.010)

There have been no cases involving the second sentence.

Section 3. Methods of Voting: Election Contests

Methods of voting, including absentee voting, shall be prescribed by law. Secrecy of voting shall be preserved. The procedure for determining election contests, with right of appeal to the courts, shall be prescribed by law.

Three important guarantees are expressed here: absentee voting must be allowed; voting must be by secret ballot; and judicial review must be provided in election contests. In all other respects, the legislature regulates voting. These general procedures are set forth in the election code (Title 15 of the Alaska Statutes).

Section 4. Voting Precincts: Registration

The legislature may provide a system of permanent registration of voters, and may establish voting precincts within election districts.

This section has been implemented by the legislature (A.S. 15.97).

Section 5. General Elections

General elections shall be held on the second Tuesday in October of every even-numbered year, but the month and day may be changed by law.

The date of general elections has been changed by the legislature to the Tuesday after the first Monday in November.

Article VI
Legislative Apportionment

Legislative apportionment refers to the distribution of house and senate seats among districts of the state. It is important politically because it determines the makeup of the legislature. A problem in all the states, but one exaggerated in Alaska because of its large size and scattered settlement, is how to provide adequate representation for sparsely settled, rural areas.

At the constitutional convention in 1955-56, a legislative apportionment scheme was devised that based house seats on population and senate seats mainly on area. Thus, it was similar to the apportionment of Congress, where each state has two senators regardless of its size or population, and a number of representatives based on its population relative to the other states.

However, in the historic 1962 case of Baker v. Carr, and in a series of other federal cases that followed, the U.S. Supreme Court declared that state systems of legislative apportionment must be based exclusively on population. The court established the rule of "one man, one vote," (now "one person, one vote") which is derived from the equal protection clause of the federal constitution. State senates apportioned on the basis of geographical area (virtually all of them) were now unconstitutional. Henceforth each senator had to represent an equal number of people. Significant deviation in the population base of each house and senate seat (greater than about 10 percent) is considered illegal unless there is compelling justification for the difference.

The effect of these court decisions was to nullify most of Article VI of Alaska's constitution. Surprisingly, there has not been an attempt made since then to amend the state constitution to rid it of obsolete material and establish new guidelines for apportionment of the senate on the basis of population. Instead, the state supreme court has had to referee each effort to reapportion the senate and to establish its own criteria for adequacy and reasonableness.[4] The Alaska supreme court has repeatedly asked the legislature to seek amendment to Article VI.

An important feature of Article VI that has remained intact in the aftermath of Baker v. Carr is the mechanism provided in Sections 8, 9, and 10 for reapportionment after each ten-year federal census. This procedure places responsibility for apportionment in the hands of the governor and a reapportionment board advisory to him. Reapportionment is traditionally a function of the legislature, but delegates at Alaska's constitutional convention were mindful of the notorious reluctance of legislatures to reapportion themselves in a fair and timely manner. Therefore, they made reapportionment an automatic process within the executive branch.

As the population of the cities in Alaska continues to grow, the rural areas lose representation in the legislature. This is the inevitable consequence of the "one person, one vote" principle. There is no constitutional remedy for it at the state level.

Section 1. Election Districts

> Members of the house of representatives shall be elected by the qualified voters of the respective election districts. Until reapportionment, election districts and the number of representatives to be elected from each district shall be as set forth in Section 1 of Article XIV.

The constitution contemplates that election districts (that is, the districts of house members) will change as the population of the state grows and its distribution shifts. An initial set of election districts was established in the constitution, but these are now obsolete.

Section 2. Senate Districts

> Members of the senate shall be elected by the qualified voters of the respective senate districts. Senate districts shall be as set forth in Section 2 of Article XIV, subject to changes authorized in this article.

This section has been obsolete since Baker v. Carr and subsequent federal court cases (see also Section 7).

---

[4]The fascinating history of reapportionment in Alaska is found in three state supreme court cases: Wade v. Nolan (444 P.2d 689; 1966), Egan v. Hammond (502 P.2d 856; 1972), and Groh v. Egan (526 P.2d 863; 1974). Doubtless the reapportionment plan adopted after the 1980 census will also be taken to the supreme court.

Section 3. Reapportionment of House
> The governor shall reapportion the house of representatives immediately following the official reporting of each decennial census of the United States. Reapportionment shall be based upon civilian population within each election district as reported by the census.

The first sentence of this section technically remains in force, although since it ignores the senate, it is now an incomplete provision and would presumably be changed by amendments that would modernize this article. It departs from tradition by giving the responsibility for reapportionment to the governor. An implication of this section is that the governor cannot reapportion between census periods even if major population changes have occurred. (This is also the implication of the last sentence of Section 10.)

The second sentence has been declared unconstitutional by the state supreme court. The convention delegates originally sought to exclude the military population from apportionment calculations because these people tended to be transients who do not vote in Alaska. Their large numbers would distort the representation of districts where military bases were located. However, the court ruled that the state must make an effort to identify those military people who do vote in Alaska and include them in the population base of the state. To do otherwise would discriminate against an entire class of individuals merely because of the nature of their employment. Also, the court ruled that reliable data other than census data could be used in making population determinations for reapportionment purposes.

Section 4. Method
> Reapportionment shall be by the methods of equal proportions, except that each election district having the major fraction of the quotient obtained by dividing total civilian population by forty shall have one representative.

Section 5. Combining Districts
> Should the total civilian population within any election district fall below one-half of the quotient, the district shall be attached to an election district within its senate district, and the reapportionment for the new district shall be determined as provided in Section 4 of this article.

These sections are obsolete. U.S. Supreme Court rulings require a nearly equal population base for each house and senate district.

Section 6. Redistricting
> The governor may further redistrict by changing the size and area of

> election districts, subject to the limitations of this article. Each new district so created shall be formed of contiguous and compact territory containing as nearly as practicable a relatively integrated socioeconomic area. Each shall contain a population at least equal to the quotient obtained by dividing the total civilian population by forty. Consideration may be given to local government boundaries. Drainage and other geographic features shall be used in describing boundaries wherever possible.

The governor must still follow these guidelines when redrawing election district boundaries. However, the third sentence must be interpreted in light of U.S. Supreme Court rulings, which require a good faith effort to achieve population equality among districts.

Section 7. Modification of Senate Districts

> The senate districts, described in Section 2 of Article XIV, may be modified to reflect changes in election districts. A district, although modified, shall retain its total number of senators and its approximate perimeter.

This section is obsolete. When the U.S. Supreme Court threw out all such fixed apportionment schemes based on area rather than population, the governor of Alaska reapportioned the senate in 1965 according to the state constitutional procedures for reapportioning the house of representatives. The state supreme court upheld his power to do so on an interim basis. Subsequent senate reapportionments have been made on this "interim" basis, as will future reapportionments until this section is formally amended.

Section 8. Reapportionment Board

> The governor shall appoint a reapportionment board to act in an advisory capacity to him. It shall consist of five members, none of whom may be public employees or officials. At least one member each shall be appointed from the Southeastern, Southcentral, Central, and Northwestern Senate Districts. Appointments shall be made without regard to political affiliation. Board members shall be compensated.

The senate districts referred to in this section no longer exist. The language indicates, however, that the drafters of the document sought broad geographical representation on the reapportionment board. The requirement that "appointments shall be made without regard to political affiliation," was intended to prevent the formulation of a reapportionment plan calculated to give partisan advantage. The words themselves, however, are ambiguous. In the case of Egan v. Hammond (505 P.2d 856; 1972), the state supreme court said the words did not mean the board must be bipartisan. However, the court said that the political affiliation of the members would certainly be a factor in determining the legitimacy of appointees to the board, as would the nature of their activities in partisan politics and their expertise and general qualifications for appointment.

Section 9. Organization

> The board shall elect one of its members chairman and may employ temporary assistants. Concurrence of three members is required for a ruling or determination, but a lesser number may conduct hearings or otherwise act for the board.

This section establishes procedures for the board, and allows it to employ a temporary staff.

Section 10. Reapportionment Plan and Proclamation

> Within ninety days following the official reporting of each decennial census, the board shall submit to the governor a plan for reapportionment and redistricting as provided in this article. Within ninety days after receipt of the plan, the governor shall issue a proclamation of reapportionment and redistricting. An accompanying statement shall explain any change from the plan of the board. The reapportionment and redistricting shall be effective for the election of members of the legislature until after the official reporting of the next decennial census.

Reapportionment is "self-executing" (that is, automatic). The reapportionment board is appointed by the governor (see Section 8), and once appointed, needs no authorization from him to begin working. The intent is to avoid the inertia that has historically slowed reapportionment. Once proclaimed by the governor, the reapportionment plan becomes law for the next ten years.

Section 11. Enforcement

> Any qualified voter may apply to the superior court to compel the governor, by mandamus or otherwise, to perform his reapportionment duties or to correct any error in redistricting or reapportionment. Application to compel the governor to perform his reapportionment duties must be filed within thirty days of the expiration of either of the two ninety-day periods specified in this article. Application to compel correction of any error in redistricting or reapportionment must be filed within thirty days following the proclamation. Original jurisdiction in these matters is hereby vested in the superior court. On appeal, the cause shall be reviewed by the supreme court upon the law and the facts.

Citizens may compel a reluctant governor to get on with reapportionment; they may also take his plan to court. The time limits specified in this and the preceding section are necessary to assure that a valid reapportionment plan exists for the statewide elections that follow soon after the U.S. census data are released.

Article VII
Health, Education, and Welfare

This article is the shortest in the constitution, and at the time it was written, the least controversial. It directs the legislature to establish a unified school system open to all children of the state; it establishes the University of Alaska; and it makes a standard, perfunctory demand for the legislature to provide for the public health and welfare.

Since its adoption, however, legal and political disputes have swirled around the public education sections of this article. This is not surprising, as public education frequently affects more people more directly and arouses more passion than any other public policy issue. The most recent controversy concerns the extent of the state's constitutional responsibility to provide secondary schools in rural villages.

A much publicized law suit, known as the Molly Hootch case, was brought on behalf of a group of Alaska Native school children to compel the state to build and operate secondary schools in their villages. Lawyers for the students argued that a school system which forced young children to leave family and home for a strange and frequently hostile environment was not one really "open to all children of the state" as contemplated by Section 1 of this article. The suit also claimed that the lack of local secondary schools in the villages amounted to racial discrimination and denial of equal protection of the laws under Article I of the Alaska Constitution and the 14th amendment of the U.S. Constitution. After much litigation (the state supreme court rejected the claims based on Section 1 of this article, and the other claims were never fully adjudicated), an out-of-court settlement was reached which required the state to pursue diligently the goal of building and operating secondary schools in rural villages.

Another well-publicized dispute turned on the meaning of the last sentence in Section 1 of this article, which prohibits the state from spending money for the "direct benefit" of private schools. Alaska had a long-standing tuition grant program that gave state residents attending private colleges in Alaska the difference between the tuition charged at their college and that charged by the state university. Opponents of the program claimed that it benefited the private schools directly although technically the grants were made to the student. To quiet the controversy, which was then in the courts, the legislature placed a constitutional amendment on the general election ballot in 1976 that would have expressly permitted the tuition grants. However, the voters rejected the proposal by a large margin. Law suits resumed, and the court declared that the grants violated the "direct benefit" clause of Section 1 because "the student is merely a conduit for the transmission of state funds to private colleges. . . ." (Sheldon Jackson College v. State, 599 P.2d 127; 1979).

Section 1. Public Education

> The legislature shall by general law establish and maintain a system of public schools open to all children of the State, and may provide for other public educational institutions. Schools and institutions so established shall be free from sectarian control. No money shall be paid from public funds for the direct benefit of any religious or other private educational institution.

At the time of statehood a dual system of public education existed in Alaska. Territorial schools served urban areas, and Bureau of Indian Affairs schools served rural Alaska Natives. By adopting this section, the people of Alaska declared it a state goal to unify this system. Two decades later, much progress has been made in achieving this goal, largely as a result of the financial strength of the state from North Slope oil revenue. Virtually all of the rural BIA schools have been taken over by state-financed local school districts. As mentioned above, the problem now is one of providing facilities and a viable program for secondary education in the smaller villages.

Section 2. State University

> The University of Alaska is hereby established as the state university and constituted a body corporate. It shall have title to all real and personal property now or hereafter set aside for or conveyed to it. Its property shall be administered and disposed of according to law.

Section 3. Board of Regents

> The University of Alaska shall be governed by a board of regents. The regents shall be appointed by the governor, subject to confirma-

tion by a majority of the members of the legislature in joint session. The board shall, in accordance with law, formulate policy and appoint the president of the university. He shall be the executive officer of the board.

These sections mandate the creation of the University of Alaska and establish certain aspects of its management. There is in this language, however, ambiguity about the degree of autonomy of the University from the executive and the legislature. A dispute between the University and the legislative and executive branches has concerned the independence of the University in allocating funds within its own budget. The governor and legislature have considered the University a state agency like any other for budgeting purposes. The University has resisted this control by the state because by allocating specific items in the budget the governor and the legislature become directly involved in the educational policies of the institution.

A state supreme court opinion on a case involving the university (University of Alaska v. National Aircraft Leasing, 536 P.2d 121; 1975) gives support to the legislative argument by declaring that the University is clearly an instrumentality of the state with its finances subject to legislative enactment, but it also upholds the autonomy of the university in a vague way by stating that it "enjoys in some limited respects a status which is co-equal rather than subordinate to that of the executive or the legislative arms of government."

Section 4. Public Health
The legislature shall provide for the promotion and protection of public health.

Section 5. Public Welfare
The legislature shall provide for public welfare.

These sections recognize the inherent and fundamental powers of the state government to protect public health and provide for the public welfare. The term "welfare" is used here in the broad and expansive sense of public well-being, not merely public assistance to the indigent and helpless.

Article VIII
Natural Resources

No other state constitution has a separate article devoted exclusively to natural resources. The presence of this article in Alaska's constitution signifies the importance of minerals, fish, and wildlife in the history of Alaska's development, and the expectation that they would continue to be significant in the future of the state. It was evident from bills pending in Congress at the time of the constitutional convention that Alaska would acquire a sizable grant of federal land when it became a state. Also, the new state would assume responsibility for the management of fish and wildlife. In their "Report to the People," the constitutional convention delegates said: "The future wealth of the State of Alaska will depend largely on how it administers the immense and the varied resources to which it will fall heir." Thus, they considered it imperative to give constitutional recognition to fundamental principles that should guide the management of the state's patrimony.

While the convention delegates sought to protect basic principles of resource management in the constitution, they also sought to avoid provisions that would be unsuitably restrictive for future generations. They were content to let future legislatures, and the courts if necessary, give contemporary meaning to general terms like public interest, maximum benefit to the people, common use, and superior public purpose. However, their aim was to fix these philosophical concepts so firmly in the law and consciousness of Alaskans that they could not be subverted by stealth, ineptitude, or inattention.

Apart from the symbolism and exhortation, what does this article really accomplish? It establishes, directly and indirectly, the following principles.

- *The natural resources of Alaska should be developed.*

The constitution clearly establishes a presumption in favor of the development and utilization of Alaska's resources. That is, development is considered desirable except when it is wasteful, destroys the ability of living resources to regenerate, violates the rights of others, is narrowly selfish and exploitive, or otherwise outrageous and offensive to the public interest. The constitution says, in effect, that there should be development but not development at any cost.

- *The natural resources of Alaska are to be managed as a public trust.*

This means that state-owned resources cannot be sold or given away in quiet deals behind closed doors. A commissioner or governor cannot, for example, secretly sell a favorite fishing spot to his friends, or a coal field to a mining company. State resources, land, and water may be sold, leased, or given away only according to principles laid down in the constitution and state law, and transactions must be in full public view. Under this article, a citizen could bring suit if he believed the legislature or the Department of Natural Resources violated the public trust in its management of the state's land, water, or wildlife resources.

- *The public should have the broadest possible access to and use of the state's natural resources.*

Article VIII emphasizes that citizens have a right to get to and use the state's resources, and that only a superior public purpose can stand in the way of this right. People can acquire rights to use state-owned land and water by purchase, lease, grant, or permit, as the legislature may prescribe.

- *Management of renewable resources must be on the basis of sustained yield.*

This means that resources such as fish, game, and timber may not be harvested faster than they can replenish themselves, so that future generations can use and enjoy the same resources. The principle of sustained yield limits the rate at which resources can be harvested. In practice, sustained yield management is difficult to achieve, but the constitution requires that it should be the objective of renewable resource programs, in contrast to maximum short-term economic return.

- *Management of state resources will recognize multiple uses whenever possible.*

Article VIII requires that state land be managed in a way that allows more than one use of an area if other uses are compatible (for example, agriculture and home sites, or mining and wildlife protection).

- *The methods of acquiring mineral rights and water rights traditionally used in Alaska and the other western states shall be preserved by the new state government to the extent allowed by Congress.*

The constitution continues the distinction between locatable and leasable minerals found in federal mining laws and continues the traditional right to appropriate water on a "first-come-first-served" basis.

- *No private property right may be created in any fishery.*

Whereas it would be theoretically possible (and perhaps economically efficient) for the state to lease the exclusive rights to all salmon in a bay or inlet just as it leases the exclusive rights to oil under certain tracts of land, the constitution prohibits this practice.

Section 1. Statement of Policy

It is the policy of the State to encourage the settlement of its land and the development of its resources by making them available for maximum use consistent with the public interest.

This is a strong statement that the policy of the state is to encourage the development of its land and resources. The qualifying phrase "consistent with the public interest" is subject to broad and changing interpretation, in much the same way that the phrase "except for a public purpose" in Article IX, Section 6 may be interpreted differently at different times. However, the words "public interest" are important because they make clear that the goal of resource development should not be pursued blindly. The early history of resource utilization in Alaska was marked by flagrant exploitation that made no lasting contribution to the development of the territory. The delegates did not consider this type of resource utilization to be in the public interest.

Section 2. General Authority
> The legislature shall provide for the utilization, development, and conservation of all natural resources belonging to the State, including land and waters, for the maximum benefit of its people.

This section is a broad grant of legislative authority to implement the policy of Section 1. Note that here, however, conservation is also added as an objective of resource management. To the authors of this section, conservation was understood in its traditional sense of "wise use." Today, the term conservation also encompasses wilderness preservation and resource protection for recreational and scientific uses.

Section 3. Common Use
> Wherever occurring in their natural state, fish, wildlife, and waters are reserved to the people for common use.

The key words in this section are "common use." On its face, it means use by everyone. But what about restrictions on common use, such as those of subsistence preference laws? The meaning of "common use" has not yet been tested in court.

Section 4. Sustained Yield
> Fish, forests, wildlife, grasslands, and all other replenishable resources belonging to the State shall be utilized, developed, and maintained on the sustained yield principle, subject to preferences among beneficial uses.

State management of renewable resources must follow the principle of sustained yield. The qualifying phrase "subject to preferences among beneficial uses" recognizes that it may be necessary to set priorities for alternative uses of a particular area of land or body of water. For example, resource managers may find that management of a forest on the basis of sustained yield conflicts with the management of deer in the same area, and that it may be necessary to decide which resource should have preference.

Section 5. Facilities and Improvements
> The legislature may provide for facilities, improvements, and services to assure greater utilization, development, reclamation, and settlement of lands, and to assure fuller utilization and development of the fisheries, wildlife, and waters.

The language of this section is, strictly speaking, unnecessary since the legislature has the inherent power to provide for all facilities, improvements, and services it deems necessary to promote a public purpose. Its presence in the constitution is hortatory—that is, it *exhorts* the legislature to do these things in order to further the constitutional mandate to utilize and develop the state's resources.

Section 6. State Public Domain

> Lands and interests therein, including submerged and tidal lands, possessed or acquired by the State, and not used or intended exclusively for governmental purposes, constitute the state public domain. The legislature shall provide for the selection of lands granted to the State by the United States, and for the administration of the state public domain.

This definition of the state public domain follows the familiar federal pattern: all state lands are in the public domain that are not explicitly withdrawn for a specific governmental purpose. The first half of the second sentence refers to land that the state was authorized to select from federally owned land in Alaska by the Alaska Statehood Act.

Section 7. Special Purpose Sites

> The legislature may provide for the acquisition of sites, objects, and areas of natural beauty or of historic, cultural, recreational, or scientific value. It may reserve them from the public domain and provide for their administration and preservation for the use, enjoyment, and welfare of the people.

This language, like that of Section 5, does not create legally enforceable rights or duties. It, too, is hortatory: it encourages the legislature to withdraw state land for these purposes, and it makes clear that such withdrawals are contemplated by the framers of the constitution even though they place heavy emphasis on development objectives in other sections.

Section 8. Leases

> The legislature may provide for the leasing of, and the issuance of permits for exploration of, any part of the public domain or interest therein, subject to reasonable concurrent uses. Leases and permits shall provide, among other conditions, for payment by the party at fault for damage or injury arising from noncompliance with terms governing concurrent use, and for forfeiture in the event of breach of conditions.

The legislature may provide for public access to resources on the public domain by leasing land for certain purposes and issuing permits for exploration. The legislature has the power to determine the length, payment, permissible uses, and any other terms and conditions of leases and permits. By the last sentence, state leases and permits must provide that the holder or his agents are responsible for damage to other resources or uses of the land which are explicitly protected by the terms of the lease or permit. Also, the state must retain the right to terminate the lease or permit if the holder violates provisions of it.

Section 9. Sales and Grants

> Subject to the provisions of this section, the legislature may provide for the sale or grant of state lands, or interests therein, and establish sales procedures. All sales or grants shall contain such reservations to the State of all resources as may be required by Congress or the State and shall provide for access to these resources. Reservation of access shall not unnecessarily impair the owners' use, prevent the control of trespass, or preclude compensation for damage.

In addition to leasing, the legislature may also sell or give away (grant) state-owned resources. "Partial interests therein" refers to a sale of mineral rights (for example, oil) on state land without selling the land itself. This section anticipated that Congress would restrict the right of the new state to sell outright its mineral land (in fact, the Statehood Act does prohibit the state from selling mineral lands). It also gives authority to the state to limit the terms of sale in any way it considers prudent to protect the public interest. One condition of sale that the state must require is that it not be denied access to abutting and adjacent lands that it owns. However, by the terms of the last sentence, this reservation of access to the state cannot be unreasonable.

Section 10. Public Notice

> No disposals or leases of state lands, or interests therein, shall be made without prior public notice and other safeguards of the public interest as may be prescribed by law.

This section prohibits the state from selling or leasing state land without a public announcement of its intention to do so. Title 38 of the Alaska Statutes, which deals with public lands, implements this section with detailed requirements for public notice and hearings prior to sale, lease, or other disposal of land.

In 1976 an amendment to this section went unsuccessfully before the voters. It proposed to add a sentence granting veto power to the legislature over all disposals of state-owned natural resources. This proposed amendment resulted mainly from legislative dissatisfaction with certain sales of state royalty oil that had been negotiated by the executive branch. At the time, many people who supported the amendment believed that its failure at the polls resulted from a biased summary of the proposition on the ballot written by individuals in the executive branch who opposed the measure.

(See discussion of Article XIII, Section 1.)

Section 11. Mineral Rights

Discovery and appropriation shall be the basis for establishing a right in those minerals reserved to the State which, upon the date of ratification of this constitution by the people of Alaska, were subject to location under the federal mining laws. Prior discovery, location, and filing, as prescribed by law, shall establish a prior right to these minerals and also a prior right to permits, leases, and transferable licenses for their extraction. Continuation of these rights shall depend upon the performance of annual labor, or the payment of fees, rents, or royalties, or upon other requirements as may be prescribed by law. Surface uses of land by a mineral claimant shall be limited to those necessary for the extraction or basic processing of the mineral deposits, or for both. Discovery and appropriation shall initiate a right, subject to further requirements of law, to patent of mineral lands if authorized by the State and not prohibited by Congress. The provisions of this section shall apply to all other minerals reserved to the State which by law are declared subject to appropriation.

Section 12. Mineral Leases and Permits

The legislature shall provide for the issuance, types and terms of leases for coal, oil, gas, oil shale, sodium, phosphate, potash, sulfur, pumice, and other minerals as many be prescribed by law. Leases and permits giving the exclusive right of exploration for these minerals for specific periods and areas, subject to reasonable concurrent exploration as to different classes of minerals, may be authorized by law. Like leases and permits giving the exclusive right of prospecting by geophysical, geochemical, and similar methods for all minerals may also be authorized by law.

These sections describe the methods by which citizens can acquire the right to mine minerals on state-owned land. They perpetuate the distinction between so-called "locatable" and "leasable" minerals in the federal mining laws. Mining interests in the territory sought to protect this familiar federal system on lands that would be transferred to the new state government. Locatable minerals are gold, silver, lead, and other metallic minerals; the main leasable minerals are coal and oil. By the terms of Section 11, a miner who discovers a metallic mineral may stake a claim that gives him the right to remove the minerals and to build a cabin and do whatever else is necessary with the land surface to develop the resource. Under federal law he could patent his claim; that is, he could get full ownership (fee title) to the land. The language in Section 11 that says "discovery and appropriation shall initiate a right, subject to further requirements of law, to patent of mineral lands if authorized by the state and not prohibited by Congress," recognizes that Congress was considering a prohibition against the new state giving patent to mineral lands. In fact, it did, and the Statehood Act forbids Alaska to alienate (that is, give full ownership rights) to state-owned mineral lands.

Section 12 provides for a system like that of the U.S. Mineral Leasing Act of 1920, whereby the rights to certain minerals are leased by the state according to any terms and conditions it may impose. Thus, for example, an oil company does not freely drill for oil on state land as a miner might dig for gold; it must first obtain from the state a lease to a certain tract, which is usually issued at a competitive auction to the person who bids the highest "bonus" (an amount over the standard payments required by the lease). Further, it must share the value of the oil it finds with the state by paying a royalty. In contrast, a gold miner may keep all of the gold he mines.

Section 13. Water Rights

> All surface and subsurface waters reserved to the people for common use, except mineral and medicinal waters, are subject to appropriation. Priority of appropriation shall give prior right. Except for public water supply, an appropriation of water shall be limited to stated purposes and subject to preferences among beneficial uses, concurrent or otherwise, as prescribed by law, and to the general reservation of fish and wildlife.

This section continues the traditional right to use water on a "first-come-first-served" basis. This method differs from an early method of acquiring water rights used historically on the East Coast. Known as the "riparian method," it allocated water rights to owners of the stream bank. In Alaska and the other western states, however, water rights were traditionally acquired by actual use of the water. Under this constitutional provision, which is further developed in state law, a prior user of water has preference to it, but his rights may be withdrawn or limited as necessary to protect public interests.

Section 14. Access to Navigable Waters

> Free access to the navigable or public waters of the State, as defined by the legislature, shall not be denied any citizen of the United States or resident of the State, except that the legislature may by general law regulate and limit such access for other beneficial uses or public purposes.

Citizens have the right to use publicly owned lakes and streams. The state may not deny this use except by a general law that protects a public interest. For example, the state may keep people away from a lake that supplies drinking water to a town, but the state may not prevent the public from fishing in a public lake because it wants to protect the interest of nearby private fishing lodges.

Section 15. No Exclusive Right of Fishery

No exclusive right or special privilege of fishery shall be created or authorized in the natural waters of the State. This section does not restrict the power of the State to limit entry into any fishery for purposes of resource conservation, to prevent economic distress among fishermen and those dependent upon them for a livelihood and to promote the efficient development of aquaculture in the State.

The second sentence of this section was added in 1972 by amendment. As originally written, the provision was intended to outlaw the use of commercial fish traps. These very efficient devices for catching salmon were permitted in southeast Alaska by the federal government over the strong objections of local fishermen who were excluded from a major portion of the salmon resource. Fish traps came to be a political symbol in the territory of federal mismanagement, corruption, and the avarice of outside commercial interests. This section, and a specific ordinance passed by the voters at the time the constitution was adopted, abolished fish traps immediately after Alaska became a state.

In the early 1970s, a proposal was advanced to limit the number of fishermen that could participate in a fishery, primarily as a way of increasing fishermen's incomes. This is the system of limited entry we have today, and because it creates a special "privilege of fishery," a constitutional amendment was necessary to allow its adoption. Aquaculture is also mentioned in the amendment so private associations may possess the right to harvest the fish they produce.

Section 16. Protection of Rights

No person shall be involuntarily divested of his right to the use of waters, his interests in lands, or improvements affecting either, except for a superior beneficial use or public purpose and then only with just compensation and by operation of law.

This section further reinforces the right of public access to state-owned resources by declaring strict conditions under which this right may be infringed or revoked. Only a superior public purpose established in law may intervene, and a fair payment must be made if a specific existing right is extinguished.

Section 17. Uniform Application

Laws and regulations governing the use or disposal of natural resources shall apply equally to all persons similarly situated with reference to the subject matter and purpose to be served by the law or regulation.

The provision seems to reassert a doctrine of "equal protection of the laws" for access to natural resources, but it also acknowledges that distinctions among groups may be necessary in the management of these resources. Groups are not always "similarly situated" with respect to fish and game resources. (The doctrine of "equal protection," of course, does not mean that everybody must be treated alike, rather that there must be a reasonable basis for different treatment.)

Section 18. Private Ways of Necessity
> Proceedings in eminent domain may be undertaken for private ways of necessity to permit essential access for extraction or utilization of resources. Just compensation shall be made for property taken or for resultant damages to other property rights.

The state may use its power of eminent domain (forcing people to sell their property to the state) for a project that is privately owned, such as an oil pipeline or a road to a mine.

Article IX
Finance and Taxation

The main constitutional issue in the area of state finances is the extent to which state and local governments should be restricted in their power to tax. Historically, state constitutions have tended to be restrictive. In the face of necessity, however, the states have devised ways to raise the money they need, including constitutional amendments exempting individual projects from debt limits; the creation of semi-autonomous public authorities to finance and operate public works; and other evasive techniques. Therefore, constitutional restrictions on taxing and spending have tended to distort state financial management, organization, and planning.

In drafting Article IX of Alaska's constitution, the committee on finance and taxation generally heeded the advice of experts and consultants who urged that the legislature be given broad discretion to tax. Apart from the usual safeguards against misappropriation of public money, the only significant constitutional restrictions in the area of public finance are those that limit state and local debt to capital improvements and require approval by the voters before this debt may be incurred. While the convention delegates generally placed great confidence in the legislature, they stopped short of allowing debt to be contracted by it alone, even on the basis of a two-thirds majority vote. Nevertheless, they did not constrain the legislature with a ceiling on state debt, curbs on rates and types of taxation, or similar limitations that appear in many older state constitutions.

Considerable public sentiment exists today for a constitutional limit on the growth of state expenditures. No thought was given to such a thing at the time of the constitutional convention, even though there was concern that the state government might be tempted to get over its head in debt providing public works. Now that the state is wealthy (temporarily at least), and the success of a legislator is measured largely by the amount of money he brings back from Juneau to his constituents, a powerful momentum of public spending inexorably builds during each session of the legislature. Many people, including a growing number of senators and representatives, regard legislative self-restraint as a will-o'-the-wisp; they see the need for a constitutional amendment on state spending to curb the relentless growth of state government. In the summer of 1981, the governor called a special session of the legislature to consider a constitutional amendment to limit spending. A proposal was adopted that will appear on the 1982 ballot for ratification.

The convention delegates included a restriction in Section 7 that is not found in many constitutions. It prohibits dedicating revenues to specific purposes. This restriction is intended to prevent the legislature from voluntarily reducing its own freedom and flexibility in financial affairs. The practice of "earmarking" revenues from certain sources for specific purposes (gasoline taxes for highway construction, for example) is common in many states (in Alabama, for example, approximately 80 percent of tax revenues are set aside for specific purposes). The consequence of dedicating tax revenue is that the legislature loses its ability to match expenditures with public needs as these change from year to year. Convention delegates believed that public needs should openly compete for state funds on a regular basis.

As originally written, the prohibition against dedicated funds in Section 7 prevented the creation of the Alaska Permanent Fund, which is a type of mandatory public savings account that receives automatic contributions from non-tax oil revenues (mainly royalties). An amendment was ratified by the voters in 1976 to authorize this popular scheme.

Section 1. Taxing Power

> The power of taxation shall never be surrendered. This power shall not be suspended or contracted away, except as provided in this article.

This is a well-established constitutional safeguard.

Section 2. Non-discrimination

> The lands and other property belonging to citizens of the United States residing without the State shall never be taxed at a higher rate than the lands and other property belonging to the residents of the State.

At the present time, neither the state nor federal constitutions tolerate different rates of taxation for residents and non-residents.

The delegates inserted this provision to reassure nonresident commercial interests (who as a group opposed statehood) that the new state government would not discriminate against them.

Section 3. Assessment Standards

> Standards for appraisal of all property assessed by the State or its political subdivisions shall be prescribed by law.

Many state constitutions require taxes to be "uniform and equal," but these provisions have complicated the fiscal life of states when courts have interpreted them to prohibit graduated income taxes, tax exemptions, and various taxing categories. Because of the potential for these problems, Alaska's constitutional convention delegates decided against a uniform and equal clause. However, they included this language to accomplish a measure of statewide uniformity in local property taxation by requiring the legislature to establish a common set of standards for assessing property.

Section 4. Exemptions

> The real and personal property of the State or its political subdivisions shall be exempt from taxation under conditions and exceptions which may be provided by law. All, or any portion of, property used exclusively for nonprofit religious, charitable, cemetery, or educational purposes, as defined by law, shall be exempt from taxation. Other exemptions of like or different kind may be granted by general law. All valid existing exemptions shall be retained until otherwise provided by law.

State and local government property is automatically exempt from taxation (this is an attribute of sovereignty). An exception to this principle contemplated in the first sentence might be a government-owned business that the legislature considers appropriate to tax, for example. The second sentence has spawned considerable litigation over the definition of "nonprofit religious, charitable, cemetery or educational purposes" by property owners seeking to qualify for the various exemptions.

Section 5. Interests in Government Property

> Private leaseholds, contracts, or interests in land or property owned or held by the United States, the State, or its political subdivisions, shall be taxable to the extent of the interests.

This section says that if a private person leases government land (to build a house on or to run a business from, for example) the value of the lease may be taxed even though the land is otherwise not taxable because the government retains ownership.

Section 6. Public Purpose

> No tax shall be levied, or appropriation of public money made, or public property transferred, nor shall the public credit be used, except for a public purpose.

This is a traditional constitutional safeguard that is, on its face, reasonable and understandable. The question is, however, what is a "public purpose"? Like the concept of the public interest, it seems to change with the times. The contemporary notion of public purpose in Alaska—which includes loan programs for private businesses and various other subsidies, welfare payments, and "longevity bonuses" (cash payments to old-timers)—is undoubtedly much broader than the view held fifty or a hundred years ago. Courts have generally given the legislature wide latitude to define public purpose. For example, the Alaska Supreme Court said, in upholding the constitutionality of the Alaska State Development Authority against a challenge on the basis of this section:

> *Where the legislature has found that a public purpose will be served by the expenditure or transfer of public funds or the use of public credit, the court will not set aside the finding of the legislature unless it clearly appears that such finding is arbitrary and without any reasonable basis in fact. (DeArmond v. Alaska State Development Corp., 376 P.2d 717; 1962).*

Section 7. Dedicated Funds

> The proceeds of any state tax or license shall not be dedicated to any special purpose, except as provided in section 15 of this article or when required by the federal government for state participation in federal programs. This provision shall not prohibit the continuance of any dedication for special purposes existing upon the date of ratification of this section by the people of Alaska.

Convention delegates prohibited the dedication, or "earmarking," of funds for specific purposes so that the legislature would not tie its own hands in providing for the public needs of the day. The phrase "as provided in section 15 of this article" in the second sentence was added by an amendment in 1976 to allow creation of the Alaska Permanent Fund (see Section 15). Two exceptions to the prohibition against earmarking were allowed by the convention delegates. One exception is a dedicated fund that was already in existence, such as the school fund of A.S. 43.50.130, which receives proceeds from the tobacco tax for use of school repair and construction. The other exception allows new earmarking when it is required by federal law to participate in a federal revenue-sharing program. This is the case with the fish and game fund of A.S. 16.05.100, to which sport hunting and license fees are dedicated.

Legal debate has surrounded the meaning of the phrase "proceeds of any state tax or license," in the first sentence. Did the authors of the constitution use the phrase to mean all state revenue, or did they want to exclude from the prohibition against dedication those state revenues that are not derived from a tax or license? The question became important when Alaska began to receive substantial income from oil lease bonuses and royalties, which are not proceeds from a tax or license.

An opinion of the attorney general of an early administration said that oil lease royalty income was outside the prohibition against earmarking in this section. A later opinion reversed this interpretation and held that the historical record of the convention made it clear that the delegates intended to bar the dedication of *all* state revenue, whether or not they derive strictly from a tax or license. Consequently, a constitutional amendment was required to create the Alaska Permanent Fund.

Note that the last sentence of Section 15 seems to permit the legislature to dedicate earnings of the Permanent Fund.

Section 8. State Debt

> No state debt shall be contracted unless authorized by law for capital improvements and ratified by a majority of the qualified voters of the State who vote on the question. The State may, as provided by law and without ratification, contract debt for the purpose of repelling invasion, suppressing insurrection, defending the State in war, meeting natural disasters, or redeeming indebtedness outstanding at the time this constitution becomes effective.

Except for meeting emergencies and paying public debts incurred during the territorial period, the legislature may incur debt only for capital improvements, and then only after approval by the voters. In the first twenty years of statehood, eighty-three bonding propositions have gone before the voters; seventy-four of these were ratified and nine rejected.

Section 9. Local Debts

> No debt shall be contracted by any political subdivision of the State, unless authorized for capital improvements by its governing body and ratified by a majority vote of those qualified to vote and voting on the question.

Local governments are also required by the constitution to limit their debt to capital projects and to secure prior approval by the voters. Capital improvements are public works of a permanent character, such as streets, sewers, schools, libraries, and public utilities.

Thus, the state supreme court ruled that the City of Juneau could not borrow money through the sale of general obligation bonds to acquire land for the expansion of state government offices, as this was not a municipal capital improvement project within the traditional meaning of the phrase. (City of Juneau v. Hixson, 373 P.2d 743; 1962).

The legislature has placed statutory limits on the taxing powers of local governments in addition to the constitutional limits of this section, such as a 3-percent (30 mills) ceiling on local property taxes.

Section 10. Interim Borrowing
> The State and its political subdivisions may borrow money to meet appropriations for any fiscal year in anticipation of the collection of the revenues for that year, but all debt so contracted shall be paid before the end of the next fiscal year.

State and local governments may engage in short-term borrowing to deal with cash-flow problems within the yearly budget cycle.

Section 11. Exceptions
> The restrictions on contracting debt do not apply to debt incurred through the issuance of revenue bonds by a public enterprise or public corporation of the State or a political subdivision, when the only security is the revenues of the enterprise or corporation. The restrictions do not apply to indebtedness to be paid from special assessments on the benefited property, nor do they apply to refunding indebtedness of the State or its political subdivisions.

General obligation bonds are backed by the full taxing power of the government that issues them. Revenue bonds are backed only by the money generated by the project they finance, such as user fees and connection charges of a sewer project, gate receipts of a sports arena, or mortgage payments of a housing authority. The restrictions in Section 9 do not apply to debt from selling this type of bond, nor to similar debts for projects that are repaid exclusively by assessments on the users.

Section 12. Budget
> The governor shall submit to the legislature, at a time fixed by law, a budget for the next fiscal year setting forth all proposed expenditures and anticipated income of all departments, offices, and agencies of the State. The governor, at the same time, shall submit a general appropriation bill to authorize the proposed expenditures, and a bill or bills covering recommendations in the budget for new or additional revenues.

Gubernatorial responsibility for preparing a budget proposal for the legislature is thought by experts to be necessary for the annual development of a comprehensive state fiscal program. It is an important element in Alaska's "strong-governor" constitutional scheme. Although the legislature retains exclusive authority to appropriate money (Section 13), this provision puts the legislature in the position of evaluating and reacting to the governor's proposed budget.

Section 13. Expenditures

> No money shall be withdrawn from the treasury except in accordance with appropriations made by law. No obligation for the payment of money shall be incurred except as authorized by law. Unobligated appropriations outstanding at the end of the period of time specified by law shall be void.

Despite the governor's initiative in preparing a budget and appropriation bill, the legislature has complete control over the spending of state funds. The last sentence of this section is an example of how the convention delegates sought to keep the constitution flexible. Most constitutions limit the life of appropriations to two years.

Section 14. Legislative Post-audit

> The legislature shall appoint an auditor to serve at its pleasure. He shall be a certified public accountant. The auditor shall conduct post-audits as prescribed by law and shall report to the legislature and to the governor.

A legislative post-audit is a review of executive agency expenditures to ensure compliance with applicable laws and regulations. A post-audit contrasts with the pre-audit used in some states where expenditures are reviewed *before* payment is made. This section makes the auditor responsible to the legislature, as a potential conflict of interest exists if the post-auditor is appointed by and responsible to the governor, as is the case in some states.

Section 15. Alaska Permanent Fund

> At least twenty-five percent of all mineral lease rentals, royalties, royalty sale proceeds, federal mineral revenue sharing payments and bonuses received by the State shall be placed in a permanent fund, the principal of which shall be used only for those income-producing investments specifically designated by law as eligible for permanent fund investments. All income from the permanent fund shall be deposited in the general fund unless otherwise provided by law.

A constitutional amendment in 1976 added this entire section. The provision mandates the creation of the Alaska Permanent Fund. This is the only fund of its type in the United States. Dedicated funds normally specify the source of the revenue and the purpose for which it is to be expended (for example, gasoline tax revenue and highway construction). This provision specifies merely that certain money will be deposited to a special fund, only the earnings of which may be spent. The fund represents a type of dedication because the deposit bypasses the legislative appropriation process. The fund's earnings are not earmarked for a particular purpose by the constitution; they are deposited in the general fund "unless otherwise provided by law." Thus, the legislature can dedicate the fund's earnings if it chooses to do so. At the present time (1981), half of the fund's earnings have been earmarked by the legislature for per capita distribution to Alaska residents.

Article X
Local Government

Like Article VIII (Natural Resources), Article X reflects considerable constitutional innovation. In drafting this article, the delegates tried to steer a middle course between too little and too much detail about local government structure. Existing constitutional provisions varied between New Jersey's silence on the subject and New York's long, discursive local government article.

Looking at metropolitan government elsewhere in the United States, the members of the local government committee saw a ragged patchwork of competing, overlapping jurisdictions. Many of these local governmental jurisdictions were single-purpose districts which were little known to the average voter. Each pursued its narrow goals without regard for broader public interests. Some obtained revenue from projects (sewer user fees, for example) and some levied taxes (fire protection districts, for example). The lack of centralized control over the activities of these numerous jurisdictions, their distance from the voter, and the absence of an integrated budget for their operations made local government inefficient and irrational in many urban areas.

Furthermore, the courts tended to construe the powers of local government very narrowly. Thus, municipal governments could not deal with pressing problems because they could not find some explicit provision of a statute or charter that authorized them to act in the area.

At the time of the convention, local government institutions were quite undeveloped in Alaska. Scattered around the territory were small cities and a few special service (e.g. school) districts. Congress had prohibited the creation of counties. It was evident that a majority of Alaskans would live in or near cities. Unincorporated areas in the Anchorage area, such as Spenard and Fairview, for example, were growing rapidly. Conflicts between special purpose districts and cities were already occurring. Things were not yet as bad as in other parts of the country, and the delegates wanted to prevent problems by limiting the number of permissible local government units.

There was general agreement on the long-term need for a unit of general purpose government between the state and the city. The delegates feared that in the absence of this intermediate level of areawide government, fiscally autonomous service districts would proliferate. This would eventually result in the chaos that made local government so inefficient and reform so difficult elsewhere. Some delegates even wanted to do away with the cities altogether and provide for a single areawide unit of local government. This idea had appeal in concept, but as a practical matter it was considered too advanced for Alaska since cities were already well established. Therefore, the convention authorized only two units of local government in the constitution, the city and the borough.

The borough was thought of as a modern, enhanced version of the traditional county. Great pains were taken to emphasize the legal and political distinctness of this new super-county form of government, including use of the term "borough" instead of county. However, the delegates were reluctant to specify anything more than the broadest constitutional framework for it. They realized that the vast differences across Alaska—differences in population distribution, concentration of taxable wealth, tradition and experience with local self-government, and so on—would require different variations of the city and borough government. Thus, Article X leaves to the legislature the task of giving specific content to the basic (if not to say abstract) constitutional scheme of borough and city government.

Article X speaks of two types of boroughs, organized and unorganized. The sparsely populated rural areas are to be provided with local government services by the legislature (Section 6) through unorganized boroughs. It is not clear how many unorganized boroughs were contemplated by the convention delegates (the intention was apparently that several would be created). In any case, the legislature has merely designated the entire area outside organized boroughs as *the* unorganized borough. Within this unorganized borough the legislature has begun to create special service districts.

A major difficulty encountered initially by the legislature in its attempt to implement Article X was the reluctance of local areas to form a new general-purpose government (the borough) in order to provide a service that was being provided by the state or by a limited, special-purpose service district. Ironically, therefore, the legislature was seen as attempting to create more government than most people wanted, and doing so in pursuit of the constitutional objective of providing "maximum local self-government with a minimum of local government units."

As events unfolded in many areas, particularly those with a single urban core, it became clear that local government could be provided most efficiently with a single unit. A movement to unify cities and boroughs emerged. Ironically, it was an effort to rationalize the two-tier constitutional scheme which was itself a far-sighted attempt to rationalize local government. In other areas, borough government has generally been accepted and relationships between boroughs, cities, and school districts have tended to stabilize, despite occasional conflicts among them.

The brief fifteen sections of this article provide a unique and flexible framework for the development of local government institutions in Alaska. The article accommodates tiny, second-class cities with only rudimentary powers of local government and the North Slope Borough, the largest (in area) and richest (in per capita tax revenue) local government unit in the United States. No substantial changes in this once-controversial article are now being seriously discussed inside or outside of the legislature. However, there are issues which may need future attention. For example, to what extent and in what forms should borough government be extended to rural, unorganized areas, and is the existing constitutional scheme flexible enough to accommodate future developments and needs in those areas?

Section 1. Purpose and Construction

> The purpose of this article is to provide for maximum local self-government with a minimum of local government units, and to prevent duplication of tax-levying jurisdictions. A liberal construction shall be given to the powers of local government units.

This succinct statement of philosophy expresses the determination of the constitution framers that Alaska have a rational, integrated, and efficient system of local government. The second sentence was included to thwart the restrictive and narrow interpretation of this article that the courts and the legislature might be tempted to give it by the weight of tradition.

Section 2. Local Government Powers

> All local government powers shall be vested in boroughs and cities. The State may delegate taxing powers to organized boroughs and cities only.

By authorizing only two units of local government—the city and the borough—the constitution seeks to avoid the proliferation of special-purpose jurisdictions. The borough is a unit of general government that can provide services outside cities as well as inside them (i.e., in the language of local government, on an "area-wide basis" and on a "non-area-wide basis").

The term borough is used to avoid linking—in the popular mind, in the action of legislators, and in the legal reasoning of judges—this new unit of local government with traditional counties.

Section 3. Boroughs
> The entire State shall be divided into boroughs, organized or unorganized. They shall be established in a manner and according to standards provided by law. The standards shall include population, geography, economy, transportation, and other factors. Each borough shall embrace an area and population with common interests to the maximum degree possible. The legislature shall classify boroughs and prescribe their powers and functions. Methods by which boroughs may be organized, incorporated, merged, consolidated, reclassified, or dissolved shall be prescribed by law.

Here the constitution says little more than that there shall be boroughs, some organized and some unorganized. It is up to the legislature to give form and content to this new creature. By implication, there are to be different classes of boroughs with different sets of powers and functions. The only guidance for creating boroughs is that the area and people have "common interests." The legislature is to establish standards for creating boroughs that shall include the general factors of "population, geography, economy, and transportation."

Also by implication, boroughs in those areas with insufficient population, wealth, and other prerequisites for local self-government are to remain "unorganized." The legislature has not created several unorganized boroughs; rather it considers all areas of the state outside of organized boroughs to be one large unorganized borough.

Section 4. Assembly
> The governing body of the organized borough shall be the assembly, and its composition shall be established by law or charter.

An amendment in 1972 to this section deleted a requirement that cities within a borough have formal representation on the borough assembly. The original provision was intended to promote cooperation between cities and boroughs and the integration of their activities. However, it violated principles of legislative apportionment enunciated in Baker v. Carr (see Article VI) and was amended to allow for apportionment of the assembly on the basis of population.

Section 5. Service Areas

> Service areas to provide special services within an organized borough may be established, altered, or abolished by the assembly, subject to the provisions of law or charter. A new service area shall not be established if, consistent with the purposes of this article, the new service can be provided by an existing service area, by incorporation as a city, or by annexation to a city. The assembly may authorize the levying of taxes, charges, or assessments within a service area to finance the special services.

The purpose of this provision is to keep the number of service areas as small as possible. It permits the creation of service areas within boroughs, but only if the service cannot be provided by an existing service area or by a city. Property receiving such services as road improvement, water supply, and fire protection from a special district may be taxed differentially to pay for them. (Sections 2 and 15 prevent the existence of autonomous service areas outside the overall jurisdiction of a borough.)

Section 6. Unorganized Boroughs

> The legislature shall provide for the performance of services it deems necessary or advisable in unorganized boroughs, allowing for maximum local participation and responsibility. It may exercise any power or function in an unorganized borough which the assembly may exercise in an organized borough.

The legislature is responsible for providing services in the unorganized borough, "allowing for maximum local participation and responsibility." In pursuit of this goal, the legislature has, for example, created special service areas (as contemplated by Section 5) in the unorganized borough. The most important of these are the rural school districts, known as regional education attendance areas, but provision has also been made for regional housing authorities and coastal management areas.

Section 7. Cities

> Cities shall be incorporated in a manner prescribed by law, and shall be a part of the borough in which they are located. Cities shall have the powers and functions conferred by law or charter. They may be merged, consolidated, classified, reclassified, or dissolved in the manner provided by law.

This section recognizes the continued existence of cities (as does Section 2), but it requires that they be "part of" a surrounding borough if one exists. The section gives broad power to the legislature to build a statutory framework for the creation and operation of cities. The constitution suggests by reference to "classification" of cities and boroughs in this and other sections that flexibility may be provided by authorizing the creation of local governments with different sets of duties and responsibilities. At the present time, two classes of cities and three classes of boroughs are recognized by statute—each with different powers.

Section 8. Council
The governing body of a city shall be the council.

Section 9. Charters
The qualified voters of any borough of the first class or city of the first class may adopt, amend, or repeal a home rule charter in a manner provided by law. In the absence of such legislation, the governing body of a borough or city of the first class shall provide the procedure for the preparation and adoption or rejection of the charter. All charters, or parts or amendments of charters, shall be submitted to the qualified voters of the borough or city, and shall become effective if approved by a majority of those who vote on the specific question.

This language gives effect to the declaration in Section 1 that the constitution provide "maximum local self government." Home rule charters—that is, locally drafted "constitutions" for local government—are the means for municipalities to exercise the largest measure of self government. "First class" municipalities (these are defined in law, not in the constitution) may adopt home rule charters. Cities and boroughs that do not have home rule charters—first class or otherwise—must operate within the limits of the powers delegated to them by the state. These are known as general law municipalities. Home rule municipalities, in contrast, may exercise all powers not explicitly denied them by state law or by their own charter (see Section 11).

Section 10. Extended Home Rule
The legislature may extend home rule to other boroughs and cities.

By the previous section the constitution extends home rule to "first class" cities and boroughs, which the legislature is to define. In this section, the convention delegates made it clear that the legislature can extend home rule to other categories of municipalities as well if it wants to do so.

Section 11. Home Rule Powers
> A home rule borough or city may exercise all legislative powers not prohibited by law or by charter.

This broad grant of home rule power is unique among state constitutions. It means that the governing body of a home rule city or borough can exercise any constitutional power of the state legislature if it is not explicitly denied by law or by the charter itself. Typically, other state constitutions narrowly enumerate the powers of home rule municipalities. With the simple and concise language of this section, the authors of Alaska's local government article sought to make the home rule power as expansive as possible. Article II, Section 19 protects home rule and other municipalities from selective intervention in their affairs by the legislature and thereby further strengthens local autonomy.

Section 12. Boundaries
> A local boundary commission or board shall be established by law in the executive branch of the state government. The commission or board may consider any proposed local government boundary change. It may present proposed changes to the legislature during the first ten days of any regular session. The change shall become effective forty-five days after presentation or at the end of the session, whichever is earlier, unless disapproved by a resolution concurred in by a majority of the members of each house. The commission or board, subject to law, may establish procedures whereby boundaries may be adjusted by local action.

Few if any other state constitutions provide for a body of this type. The independent authority of this agency to establish the borders of local government units, subject only to legislative veto, recognizes that the most "rational" boundaries may not always result from the local tug and tussle of politics. In the words of the convention committee on local government, this scheme allows boundary decisions to be made "at a level where area-wide or statewide needs can be taken into account. By placing authority in this third party, arguments for and against boundary change can be analyzed objectively." In its deliberations, the local boundary commission must refer to the standards for borough and city formation established by the legislature .

The veto power (exercised here by a simple majority of both houses acting separately) has been exercised freely by the legislature over decisions of the commission.

Section 13. Agreements; Transfer of Powers
> Agreements, including those for cooperative or joint administration

> of any functions or powers, may be made by any local government with any other local government, with the State, or with the United States, unless otherwise provided by law or charter. A city may transfer to the borough in which it is located any of its powers or functions unless prohibited by law or charter, and may in like manner revoke the transfer.

Convention delegates sought to minimize the duplication of services provided by cities and boroughs. By this and the original language in Section 4 (since removed by amendment), the constitution seeks cooperation and the fullest reasonable integration of activities between cities and boroughs. This section is intended to facilitate an efficient division of labor between the city and borough by various means, including transfer of functions from the city to the borough. This section also includes general enabling provisions for cooperative intergovernmental relations at the state and federal levels.

Section 14. Local Government Agency

> An agency shall be established by law in the executive branch of the state government to advise and assist local governments. It shall review their activities, collect and publish local government information, and perform other duties prescribed by law.

The agency prescribed by this section is the Department of Community and Regional Affairs (formerly the Local Affairs Agency). It is the only executive agency mandated by the constitution. Its presence here symbolizes both the importance placed on local government matters by the constitution's authors and the state interest they saw in fostering strong local self-government.

Section 15. Special Service Districts

> Special service districts existing at the time a borough is organized shall be integrated with the government of the borough as provided by law.

Those at the convention who wanted independent school districts to remain autonomous after statehood were defeated by the inclusion of this section. In keeping with the general constitutional objectives of minimizing local jurisdictions and favoring general purpose over special purpose government, the delegates voted to require school districts to be absorbed by boroughs. Under this scheme, the borough levies taxes to support education and approves the budget of the school district, which otherwise continues under the management of a local school board and separate school administration. Within general tax and budget restraints, borough school districts have substantial autonomy.

Article XI
The Initiative, Referendum, and Recall

The initiative and referendum are devices that permit the electorate to participate directly in the law-making process. By initiative the voters may enact legislation, and by the referendum they may veto legislation passed by the legislature. The recall allows the voters to remove an elected official from office during his term. The initiative and referendum are known as "direct democracy" or "direct legislation" provisions. They originated from the populist reform movement of the early twentieth century, and they are found in one form or another in about half of the state constitutions.

Procedures for using the initiative and referendum are specified in this article, whereas the procedures and grounds for recalling elected officials are left entirely to the legislature. Generally speaking, Alaska's convention delegates were ambivalent about direct democracy, for while they authorized it on the one hand, they greatly restricted its use on the other. Constitutional hedges on the use of the initiative and referendum reflect faith on the part of convention delegates in the wisdom and responsibility of the legislature, fear on the part of some delegates that these devices would be exploited by special interests for their own narrow purposes, and outright suspicion by others of the passions and impulses of the voters.

By 1980, nine initiative measures had gone before the voters, five of which were adopted. One of these was a curious variation of the initiative concept not foreseen in the language of Article XI insofar as it did not enact a law. This was an "advisory" vote to the legislature regarding a constitutional amendment to create a unicameral (one house) legislature. Since Article XIII, Section 1 precludes the use of the initiative to amend the constitution, and since the legislature refused to place a unicameral amendment before the voters, backers of unicameralism did what they could to bring pressure on the legislature by initiating an advisory ballot proposition. Although technically an initiative, this measure was loosely referred to as a "referendum" on the question of unicameralism. The "advisory vote" took another twist in 1978 when the legislature itself placed a ballot proposition before the voters seeking guidance on the constitutional question of limiting the length of legislative sessions.[5] This, too, was loosely referred to as a "referendum," but it was neither an initiative nor a referendum as described by Article XI.

Legislation brought about by initiative is similar to laws of the legislature in all respects. It is subject to judicial review. In fact, one of the five initiated laws in Alaska's twenty-year history was declared unconstitutional by the state supreme court because it violated certain restrictions on the use of the initiative provided in Section 7 of this article.

In contrast to the relatively frequent use of the initiative, the referendum has been used only once in the first twenty years of statehood. A portion of the referendum was declared unconstitutional by the state supreme court. The referred law was a general state pay raise that included legislators' salaries and retirement benefits. It went into effect before it was repealed by the voters (see Section 5). Contributions were made to the new retirement system during the intervening months. Since Article XII, Section 7, prohibits retirement benefits from being decreased, the supreme court ruled that the referendum could not veto this aspect of the pay bill.

On two other occasions voters have passed judgment on laws enacted by the legislature, but these laws were submitted by the legislature itself rather than by citizen action through the referendum provisions of Article XI. A 1968 act providing for preregistration of voters and a 1980 act creating the Alaska Statehood Commission both contained requirements that the electorate give its approval before the laws became effective. Each of these ballot propositions was called a referendum, although neither was a constitutional referendum under the terms of Article XI. Two other propositions have appeared on the ballot as referendums, but these concern the convening of a constitutional convention and are authorized by Article XII of the constitution.

---

[5]Advocates of a session limit could muster only a simple majority to bring about the advisory vote and not the two-thirds majority necessary to place a constitutional amendment on the ballot. By seeking an expression of public sentiment (the measure passed overwhelmingly) the advocates of a session limit hoped to bring pressure on the legislators who opposed the measure.

Section 1. Initiative and Referendum
> The people may propose and enact laws by the initiative, and approve or reject acts of the legislature by the referendum.

The people can accomplish by the initiative what the legislature can accomplish by enacting laws, except for the explicit limitations in Section 7 of this article. Likewise, the people cannot accomplish by the initiative anything the legislature is prohibited from doing.

Only "acts of the legislature" may be repealed by the referendum. Therefore, presumably, the referendum could not be used to repeal initiated legislation. The referendum is essentially similar to the veto power of the governor. Therefore, for example, it applies to entire acts, not portions of them.

In the opinion of the attorney general, the initiative may be used to repeal laws if the referendum is not available because of constitutional restrictions on its use. Thus, the people could use the initiative to repeal a law that was enacted by initiative, or when the 90-day period of Section 5 had expired, or if rejection of only part of the law were sought. An initiative was certified for the ballot that sought to repeal the state's limited entry law which had been standing for several years. The initiative was defeated in the 1976 general election. An initiative that would repeal the state's subsistence law has been certified for the 1982 general election.

Section 2. Application
> An initiative or referendum is proposed by an application containing the bill to be initiated or the act to be referred. The application shall be signed by not less than one hundred qualified voters as sponsors, and shall be filed with the lieutenant governor. If he finds it in proper form, he shall so certify. Denial of certification shall be subject to judicial review.

This is the first step of a two-step process of placing an initiative or referendum on the ballot. It requires an application signed by 100 qualified voters. This step assures that the measure has some popular support before the state goes to the expense of printing petitions. Also, it creates a threshold level of effort to discourage entirely frivolous petitions.

Section 3. Petition
> After certification of the application, a petition containing a summary of the subject matter shall be prepared by the lieutenant governor for circulation by the sponsors. If signed by qualified voters, equal in number to ten percent of those who voted in the preceding general election and resident in at least two-thirds of the election districts of the State, it may be filed with the lieutenant governor.

This is the second and more difficult step in securing a place on the ballot for an initiative or referendum. In the 1980 general election, 162,653 people voted, so an initiative or referendum petition would require 16,266 signatures from two-thirds of the election districts to be placed on the 1982 ballot.

These requirements guarantee substantial and widespread support for an initiative or referendum before it reaches the ballot. There has been debate at times over the question of whether the requirements are too stringent. Amendments have been suggested, but never brought before the electorate, to reduce the number of signatures to five percent of the voters in the preceding election. The constitutional convention hotly debated this question, and decided on 10 percent as a compromise between 8 percent suggested by some and 15 percent suggested by others.

Section 4. Initiative Election
> An initiative petition may be filed at any time. The lieutenant governor shall prepare a ballot title and proposition summarizing the proposed law, and shall place them on the ballot for the first statewide election held more than one hundred twenty days after adjournment of the legislative session following the filing. If, before the election, substantially the same measure has been enacted, the petition is void.

There is the possibility that an initiative petition may be written by people who are unfamiliar with the finer points of bill drafting or the relationship of their bill to other legislation. Also, it may do something the legislature does not want to do, or at least not in the manner contemplated by the initiative petition. This section gives the legislature an opportunity to consider fully the subject matter of an initiative petition and adopt its own version of an initiated bill before it goes on the ballot. This procedure was designed to incorporate features of the "indirect initiative," by which voters can introduce bills in the legislature.

If the legislature passes a bill that is "substantially the same" as an initiative, the petition dies. This has happened twice in the twenty years since statehood, once in 1974 with an act regulating election campaign financing (see Warren v. Boucher, 543 P.2d 731; 1975) and again in 1979 with an act repealing the state's personal income tax. (Needless to say, sponsors of the initiatives which were set aside did not think the measures passed by the legislature were substantially the same as their own.) State statutes provide that this determination is made by the lieutenant governor with a formal concurrence of the attorney general. Also, the statutes require that the lieutenant governor's review of initiative petitions include a determination of whether subjects are included that are prohibited by Section 7 (see A.S. 15.45.010).

Section 5. Referendum Election

> A referendum petition may be filed only within ninety days after adjournment of the legislative session at which the act was passed. The lieutenant governor shall prepare a ballot title and proposition summarizing the act and shall place them on the ballot for the first statewide election held more than one hundred eighty days after adjournment of that session.

An aggrieved voter has three months from the end of the session to collect all the signatures necessary to refer a bill to the electorate (a referendum campaign could begin as soon as the bill was passed, thus allowing more than 90 days in some cases). Some state constitutions provide for the suspension of the legislative act when a referendum application has been filed against it, pending the outcome of the election. However, Alaska's constitution allows the law to take effect and, by the terms of Section 6, stay in effect for thirty days after the defeat of the measure at the polls.

If the voters wished to repeal an act or a part of it after the 90-day deadline, they would have to file an initiative petition (see commentary on Section 1).

Section 6. Enactment

> If a majority of the votes cast on the proposition favor its adoption, the initiated measure is enacted. If a majority of the votes cast on the proposition favor the rejection of an act referred, it is rejected. The lieutenant governor shall certify the election returns. An initiated law becomes effective ninety days after certification, is not subject to veto, and may not be repealed by the legislature within two years of its effective date. It may be amended at any time. An act rejected by referendum is void thirty days after certification. Additional procedures for the initiative and referendum may be prescribed by law.

Particularly interesting in this section is what is said about repealing and amending an initiated law, and what is not said about readopting a law vetoed by a referendum. While the constitution prevents the legislature from repealing an initiated act for two years after its effective date, it allows the legislature to amend it at any time. In effect, this puts initiated laws at the mercy of the legislature. (An opinion of the attorney general states: "Even though a particular amendment might clearly 'gut' an initiative and amount to destruction of the initiators' general intent, the power to effectively 'destroy' an act on a piecemeal basis resides in the legislature.") Also, there is nothing in the constitution to prevent the legislature from passing again a law vetoed by referendum. Unlike a governor's veto, the referendum is an arduous, burdensome, expensive, and time-consuming process, and once done it is unlikely to be redone on the same legislation. Thus, in the event an initiated law or a veto by referendum is especially offensive to the legislature, political pressure rather than constitutional law deters the legislature from overturning it.

Section 7. Restrictions

> The initiative shall not be used to dedicate revenues, make or repeal appropriations, create courts, define the jurisdiction of courts or prescribe their rules, or enact local or special legislation. The referendum shall not be applied to dedications of revenue, to appropriations, to local or special legislation, or to laws necessary for the immediate preservation of the public peace, health, or safety.

The initiative and referendum are expressly prohibited from being used for certain purposes. That certain subjects are off limits to direct democracy reveals the doubts of the convention delegates that the electorate could be entirely trusted to act intelligently and dispassionately. They believed that reasoned, responsible action was more likely to result from the deliberations of the people's representatives.

One initiated law ran afoul of a provision in this section and was declared unconstitutional by the state supreme court. In 1978, an initiated law required the state to distribute parcels of land to residents. The court ruled that land was an asset of the state treasury comparable to money and therefore could not be appropriated by initiative. The purpose of the constitutional prohibition against appropriating public funds is to prevent the voters from adopting ill-conceived give-away programs. The court said that "the lure of an immediate grant of land poses the same temptation as an immediate grant of money. Both decisions . . . require the reasoned deliberation characteristic of legislation action" (Thomas v. Baily, 595 P.2d 1; 1979).

Although use of the initiative to place constitutional amendments before the voters is not expressly forbidden in this section, it is precluded by Article XIII, which authorizes only two methods to amend the constitution, and by Section 1 of this article which limits the use of the initiative to enacting laws.

Section 8. Recall

> All elected public officials in the State, except judicial officers, are subject to recall by the voters of the State or political subdivision

> from which elected. Procedures and grounds for recall shall be prescribed by the legislature.

The governor, lieutenant governor, and legislators are subject to popular recall by this section. Legislators can be recalled only by the voters of the district that elected them. Procedures for use of the recall are specified in A.S. 15.14. These include the grounds for recall, which are: lack of fitness, incompetence, neglect of duties, or corruption. The legislature has also authorized the recall of elected municipal officials in the state municipal code (A.S. 29).

Article XII
General Provisions

A number of constitutional odds and ends are contained in this article. During the convention the delegates referred to it as the "miscellaneous article." Items were included that did not fit logically in any other article.

Several of the provisions of the article were included in anticipation of the requirements Congress would make on Alaska as a condition of admission to the United States. The delegates wanted a document fully acceptable to Congress that would take effect immediately upon the formal declaration of statehood. They consulted other state constitutions and drafts of pending statehood legislation for guidance in drafting these provisions. Sections 1, 4, 5 and 12 are the result of this effort. Section 13 constituted agreement in advance to any terms and conditions Congress might impose on the new state of Alaska.

Other provisions of the article define words and phrases used elsewhere in the document, clarify intent, mandate a merit system for state employment, and protect retirement benefits of former state workers.

Section 1. State Boundaries
> The State of Alaska shall consist of all the territory, together with the territorial waters appurtenant thereto, included in the Territory of Alaska upon the date of ratification of this constitution by the people of Alaska.

Here the boundaries of the State of Alaska are recognized. There had been talk in Washington, D.C. of partitioning Alaska and granting statehood only to the southern half, which seemed to have the best prospects for economic viability, but the idea was never seriously considered. Thus, this provision is not so much a denunciation of this partition idea as it was a formal definition of the boundaries of the state.

Section 2. Intergovernmental Relations
> The State and its political subdivisions may cooperate with the United States and its territories, and with other states and their political subdivisions on matters of common interest. The respective legislative bodies may make appropriations for this purpose.

The theme of intergovernmental cooperation in this article reflects the public relations function of the document discussed above in "The Background of Alaska's Constitution." It is a pious declaration of friendship, as all states have the power to engage in cooperation of the type discussed in this section without an enabling provision. (International political relationships are, of course, exclusively a federal matter.)

Section 3. Office of Profit.
> Service in the armed forces of the United States or of the State is not an office or position of profit as the term is used in this constitution.

Serving in the U.S. military or national guard does not disqualify a person from becoming a legislator under Article II, Section 5, or governor or lieutenant governor under Article III, Section 6.

Section 4. Disqualification for Disloyalty
> No person who advocates, or who aids or belongs to any party or organization or association which advocates the overthrow by force or violence of the government of the United States or of the State shall be qualified to hold any public office of trust or profit under this constitution.

This section is derived from statehood bills pending at the time of the convention.

Section 5. Oath of Office
> All public officers, before entering upon the duties of their offices, shall take and subscribe to the following oath or affirmation: "I do solemnly swear (or affirm) that I will support and defend the Constitution of the United States and the Constitution of the State of Alaska, and that I will faithfully discharge my duties as ─────
> to the best of my ability." The legislature may prescribe further oaths or affirmations.

This, too, is a provision that derived from pending statehood legislation.

Section 6. Merit System

> The legislature shall establish a system under which the merit principle will govern the employment of persons by the State.

The constitution here mandates a "merit system" for state employment. A state civil service keeps state jobs from becoming the political spoils of office, and it encourages the development of a competent, permanent workforce. All permanent employees are included in the state's system except the top positions in each executive department (including the governor's office) and the Legislative Affairs Agency. The state's personnel system is set out in detail in Title 39 of the Alaska Statutes.

Section 7. Retirement Systems

> Membership in employee retirement systems of the State or its political subdivisions shall constitute a contractual relationship. Accrued benefits of these systems shall not be diminished or impaired.

Retired state workers are protected by this section from the loss or reduction of retirement benefits due them.

Section 8. Residual Power

> The enumeration of specified powers in this constitution shall not be construed as limiting the powers of the State.

The state receives the same protection here that individuals receive from Article I, Section 21. The provision is not technically necessary, as it is established legal doctrine in the United States that a state may exercise all the powers not denied it in the U.S. Constitution or its own state constitution.

Section 9. Provisions Self-executing

> The provisions of this constitution shall be construed to be self-executing whenever possible.

A "self-executing" provision is one that takes effect without implementation by legislative or executive action. The purpose of this section is to lessen the opportunity for the legislature or the governor to stand between the people and the constitution.

Section 10. Interpretation

> Titles and subtitles shall not be used in construing this constitution. Personal pronouns used in this constitution shall be construed as including either sex.

Titles such as "Article XII, General Provisions," and subtitles such as "Section 10 Interpretation" have no legal meaning in the constitution. The second sentence of this provision means that the words *he* and *his* also mean *she* and *her*.

Section 11. Law-making Power

> As used in this constitution, the terms "by law" and "by the legislature," or variations of these terms, are used interchangeably when related to law-making powers. Unless clearly inapplicable, the law-making powers assigned to the legislature may be exercised by the people through the initiative, subject to the limitations of Article XI.

The first sentence equates the terms *by law* and *by the legislature*. The second sentence makes it clear that the initiative can only be used to enact laws, as limited by Article XI, Section 7. Thus, for example, the initiative may not be used to amend the constitution.

Section 12. Disclaimer and Agreement

> The State of Alaska and its people forever disclaim all right and title in or to any property belonging to the United States, or subject to its disposition, and not granted or confirmed to the State or its political subdivisions, by or under the act admitting Alaska to the Union. The State and its people further disclaim all right or title in or to any property, including fishing rights, the right or title to which may be held by or for any Indian, Eskimo, or Aleut, or community thereof, as that right or title is defined in the act of admission. The State and its people agree that, unless otherwise provided by Congress, the property, as described in this section, shall remain subject to the absolute disposition of the United States. They further agree that no taxes will be imposed upon any such property, until otherwise provided by the Congress. This tax exemption shall not apply to property held by individuals in fee without restrictions on alienation.

With the exception of the second sentence, this provision is the conventional *clause irrevocable* which is found in virtually all statehood acts since Ohio's. Its purpose is to avoid land disputes between new states and the federal government. Section 8 of the Alaska Statehood Act contains similar language, and these two statements constitute a form of contract between the federal government and the people of the State of Alaska.

The novel feature of this provision and its counterpart in Section 8 of the Statehood Act is the reference to Native rights. The purpose of this reference was to leave open the possibility of Alaska Natives receiving compensation from the federal government for their claims to land in Alaska. It took a special act of Congress, the Alaska Native Claims Settlement Act of 1971, to settle the matter of Native land claims. In the meantime, the federal government suspended the right of the State of Alaska to select its land entitlement under the Statehood Act because the claims of the Natives conflicted with the state's land selections.

Section 13. Consent to Act of Admission

> All provisions of the act admitting Alaska to the Union which reserve rights or powers to the United States, as well as those prescribing the terms or conditions of the grants of lands or other property, are consented to fully by the State and its people.

By this section the people of Alaska gave advance consent to the terms of the future Statehood Act, whatever they might be. Advance consent to terms of the Statehood Act regarding mineral rights is found in Article VIII, Sections 9 and 11. Giving blanket consent to the Statehood Act was a controversial issue at the constitutional convention, but it was finally agreed to because the delegates knew that Congress would require consent by Alaskans to the statehood bill and because the likely terms of admission had already become apparent in pending statehood legislation. The delegates hoped that this provision would substitute for a special referendum to ratify the future Statehood Act, but in fact, the Statehood Act did require Alaskans to go to the polls and vote to approve the Act. This vote occurred on August 26, 1958, and 85 percent of the ballots cast favored admission under the terms of the Act.

Article XIII
Amendment and Revision

The authors of Alaska's constitution sought to reduce the need for amendments by leaving to the legislature many matters that are typically included in the constitutions of other states, such as the powers of local government and organization of the executive branch. They also provided automatic mechanisms to deal with anticipated changes, such as legislative reapportionment. Thus, the authors tried to write a constitution that would not invite or require the annual tampering that has made monsters of many state constitutions.

Article XIII provides for the formal amendment of the constitution. The convention delegates sought to make the amendment procedures difficult enough to prevent hasty, destructive, and cluttering changes, but easy enough to allow the constitution to accommodate the legitimate needs of a changing society. Because constitutional matters are of a fundamental importance, the convention delegates believed that all changes should be ratified by the voters (only the constitution of Delaware may be amended without a vote of the people). To ensure that changes are well-conceived and properly drafted, the convention required a two-step process that would allow for adequate deliberation, attention to detail, and the opportunity for reflection. Thus, proposals for change must emerge from a deliberative body (step one) before they reach the electorate for ratification (step two). The deliberative body may be either the legislature or a constitutional convention convened expressly for the purpose of studying changes in the state's basic law. Thus, the delegates did not allow the constitution to be amended by the initiative process because that process bypasses a deliberative body.

As the governmental body is broadly representative of the people, the legislature is the logical and traditional point of origin for proposed amendments. But to ensure that proposed amendments command substantial support, the constitution requires a two-thirds majority to bring them before the voters.

The legislature should not be the only source of proposals for change, however, because legislatures are frequently slow to reform themselves or to curtail their own power. Furthermore, the legislature is not the right place to give the constitution a major overhaul if one is needed; this is properly the job of a body dedicated specifically to that task and equipped for it.

For these reasons, the delegates made explicit provision for constitutional conventions. According to Article XIII, a convention may be convened at any time by the legislature, but the voters of the state may decide for themselves every ten years whether a convention should be called. Also, the people may exercise the legislature's discretion to convene a convention at any time through the initiative process.

Thus did the scheme for amending Alaska's constitution take shape at the convention at Fairbanks in 1955-56. Note that the governor has no role in it. The governor may not veto an amendment adopted in the legislature. (Proposed amendments are presented in the legislature as resolutions, not bills, and the governor's veto power pertains only to bills.) Nor may the governor propose amendments and place them directly on the ballot. As a consequence of this exclusion from the amending process, the governor is disadvantaged in periodic struggles with the legislature over constitutional issues pertaining to the separation of powers. For example, between 1976 and 1980, seven of nine constitutional amendments placed on the ballot by the legislature were designed to enhance legislative authority, in most cases at the expense of executive authority. (Six of the seven were defeated by the voters, however.)

The provisions of Article XIII seem to have worked reasonably well in their first two decades of use. The constitution has been amended sixteen times.[6] Seven amendment proposals have been rejected by voters. Approximately 290 resolutions have been introduced in the legislature proposing constitutional change, many of these the same proposal or a variation of the same proposal, such as an elected attorney general, unicameralism, etc. A convention to review the constitution has not yet been held (see Section 3).

Section 1. Amendments

Amendments to this constitution may be proposed by a two-thirds vote of each house of the legislature. The lieutenant governor shall

[6]See Appendix A.

> prepare a ballot title and proposition summarizing each proposed amendment, and shall place them on the ballot for the next general election. If a majority of the votes cast on the proposition favor the amendment, it shall be adopted. Unless otherwise provided in the amendment, it becomes effective thirty days after the certification of the election returns by the lieutenant governor.

Alaska's constitution may be amended by two methods. This section authorizes the legislature to propose amendments to the electorate by two-thirds majority in each house. The remaining sections of this article deal with the second method of amendment, the constitutional convention.

This section was amended in 1974 by substituting the word "general" for "statewide" near the end of the second sentence. As a result of this change, proposed constitutional amendments appear on the general election ballot rather than the primary election ballot (the primary is the first statewide election to occur after the end of a regular legislative session). There is normally a higher voter turn-out for general elections than for primary elections (for example, in 1980, 59 percent more votes were cast in the general than in the primary election).

In 1976 a dispute occurred between the legislature and the executive over the objectivity of the summary of a proposed amendment that was written for the ballot by the lieutenant governor. The legislature was bitterly angry that the wording of the summary biased voters against the proposal, which failed at the polls. If ratified, the amendment would have required legislative approval of sales and leases of state-owned resources made by the Department of Natural Resources. This "legislative veto" was opposed by the executive branch as a violation of the separation of powers, and the wording on the ballot suggested that the proposal sought illegal objectives.[7] To prevent recurrence of charges of biased ballot summaries, the legislature established in law a mechanism for the review of ballot wording, including the opportunity for judicial review (A.S. 15.50.025).

Section 2. Convention

> The legislature may call constitutional conventions at any time.

By implication, the voters may also call a constitutional convention at any time. This is because the voters can do by initiative what

---

[7]The ballot summary stated, in part: "The amendment would, with respect to state land disposals, exempt the legislature from the constitutional prohibition against local and special legislation, vest the legislature with the veto power and vest the legislature with the executive power of administration and the judicial power of review."

the legislature can do unless explicitly denied in the constitution, and calling a convention by initiative is not denied in Article XI, Section 7 (see also Article XII, Section 11).

Section 3. Call by Referendum

> If during any ten-year period a constitutional convention has not been held, the lieutenant governor shall place on the ballot for the next general election the question: "Shall there be a Constitutional Convention?" If a majority of the votes cast on the question are in the negative, the question need not be placed on the ballot until the end of the next ten-year period. If a majority of the votes cast on the question are in the affirmative, delegates to the convention shall be chosen at the next regular statewide election, unless the legislature provides for the election of the delegates at a special election. The secretary of state shall issue the call for the convention. Unless other provisions have been made by law, the call shall conform as nearly as possible to the act calling the Alaska Constitutional Convention of 1955, including, but not limited to, number of members, districts, election and certification of delegates, and submission and ratification of revisions and ordinances. The appropriation provisions of the call shall be self-executing and shall constitute a first claim on the state treasury.

This is an automatic provision of the constitution that guarantees to the voters a chance to decide at least once every ten years if a constitutional convention should be held. Alaska is the only state that uses a ten-year interval. Among the few states with a similar provision, a twenty-year interval between referenda on a convention is used. Delegates to the convention chose ten years on the grounds that change would be occuring fast in Alaska. This section specifies procedures for holding a convention in order to prevent the legislature from thwarting the will of the voters by refusing to issue a call or to appropriate funds for the convention.

The first referendum on the question of holding a constitutional convention is an interesting episode in Alaska's political and constitutional history. On schedule in 1970, the question was put to a vote. The ballot read: "As required by the constitution of the State of Alaska Article XIII, Section 3, shall there be a constitutional convention?" The outcome was a very narrow affirmative vote, 34,911 to 34,472. However, opponents of the convention sued, claiming that the wording of the ballot proposition biased the vote in favor of the measure by implying that the convention, rather than the vote, was required by the constitution. The courts agreed and threw out the election results (see Boucher v. Bomhoff, 495 P.2d 77; 1972). The question was put before the voters again at the next general election (1972) with the constitutionally-required language, "Shall there be a constitutional convention?", and it was strongly defeated (29,192 to 55,389). This question will again be put before the voters in 1982.

Section 4. Powers

> Constitutional conventions shall have plenary power to amend or revise the constitution, subject only to ratification by the people. No call for a constitutional convention shall limit these powers of the convention.

The power of a convention to propose constitutional changes cannot be limited ("plenary" means full). Thus, for example, the legislature may not call a constitutional convention to consider only one or two articles, or to consider any changes except unicameralism.

Article XV[8]
Schedule of Transitional Measures

The text of Article XV appears in Appendix C. Primarily, this article establishes the legal continuity between the territory and the state of Alaska and sets in motion the new machinery of state government. Because it deals with transitional matters which are now history, this article is no longer a working part of the constitution. Indeed, the courts have ruled that provisions of Article XV may be amended by statute, and it is therefore technically not part of the constitution. A future comprehensive revision of the constitution should drop this article from the document.

Interestingly, Section 20 of Article XV declares the capital of the state to be Juneau. Placing this provision in the transitional articles rather than in the body of the constitution represents a major compromise made by delegates at the constitutional convention. Location of the capital was perhaps the most divisive of all the issues facing the delegates, and they finally agreed to postpone the issue by putting Section 20 in the transitional article. At the time, however, the consequences of doing so were not altogether clear, and it required a court case (State v. Hagglund, 374 P.2d 316; 1962) to establish that the provisions in Article XV could be changed by statute rather than the constitutional amendment process. (In this case, the question was whether the people could change Section 20 by initiative, and the state supreme court said yes.)

Article XI also contains a provision for three ordinances to be ratified by the electorate: the first concerned the constitution itself; the second concerned the adoption of the Alaska-Tennessee Plan;

---

[8]Article XIV, the current apportionment schedule, is presented in Appendix B. The original apportionment schedule has been modified since its adoption by the constitutional convention and is now obsolete. Note that the current schedule has been adopted by procedures which are not part of the constitution (see introductory discussion of Article V).

and the third concerned the abolition of fish traps in Alaska.

Adoption of the Alaska-Tennessee Plan meant that the voters would elect two "shadow" senators and a representative who would go to Washington, D.C., and lobby for statehood. While they would not have any legal power, they would be a constant reminder to Congress of the aspirations of Alaskans for admission to the Union.

Fish traps in the territory had become a symbol of nonresident exploitation of Alaska. These efficient fishing devices were owned by canneries and allowed to operate by the federal government. Local people opposed them because they excluded individual fishermen from a large portion of the salmon harvest in southeast Alaska, and they were thought to be harmful to the fishery resource as well. (The history of fish traps in Alaska is summarized in the early supreme court case of Metlakatla Indian Community, Annette Island Reserve v. Egan, 362 P.2d 901; 1961). The proposed ordinance prohibited the use of fish traps. This ordinance would become effective as soon as Alaska achieved statehood.

Voters ratified all three ordinances: they approved the constitution by a vote of 17,447 to 8,180; they endorsed the Alaska-Tennessee Plan 15,011 to 9,556; and they voted to abolish fish traps by 21,285 to 4,004.

Appendices

APPENDIX A

List of All Constitutional Amendments through 1980

Year of Legislative Action	Title	Legislative Reference	Election Date	Certification Date	Effective[9] Date	Provisions Affected
1966	Permits voting requirements for President and Vice President to be set by law.	SJR 1	Aug. 23, 1966	Sept. 9, 1966	Oct. 9, 1966	Article V, sec. 1
1968	Creates commission on judicial qualifications.	2d FCCS SCS CSHJR74	Aug. 27, 1968	Sept. 11, 1968	Oct. 11, 1968	Article IV, sec. 10, 13
1968	Pertaining to compensation of commission on judicial qualifications.	2d FCCS SCS CSHJR74	Aug. 27, 1968	Sept. 11, 1968	Oct. 11, 1968	Article IV, sec. 13
1969	Sets voting age at 18 years.	HJR 7	Aug. 25, 1970	Sept. 10, 1970	Oct. 10, 1970	Article V, sec. 1
1970	Changes title of secretary of state to lieutenant governor	SJR 2	Aug. 25, 1970	Sept. 10, 1970	Oct. 10, 1970	Article III, sec. 7-11, 13-15, 25; Article XI, sec. 2-6; Article XIII, sec. 1,3
1970	Provides for election of chief justice by majority of supreme court.	FCCS SCS CSHJR 11	Aug. 25, 1970	Sept. 10, 1970	Oct. 10, 1970	Article IV, sec. 2, 16
1970	Places executive director of the court system under the control of the entire supreme court.	FCCS SCS CSHJR 11	Aug. 25, 1970	Sept. 10, 1970	Oct. 10, 1970	Article IV, sec. 16

Year	Description	Bill	Date 1	Date 2	Date 3	Article
1970	Eliminates requirement to read or speak English for voting.	HJR 51 am S	Aug. 25, 1970	Sept. 10, 1970	Oct. 10, 1970	Article V, sec. 1
1971	Amends exclusive right of fisheries provision	HCS CSSJR 10	Aug. 22, 1972	Sept. 14, 1972	Oct. 14, 1972	Article VIII, sec. 3
1972	Includes "sex" in civil rights provision	HJR 102	Aug. 22, 1972	Sept. 14, 1972	Oct. 14, 1972	Article I, sec. 3
1972	Guarantees right to privacy.	HCS SJR 68	Aug. 22, 1972	Sept. 14, 1972	Oct. 14, 1972	Article I, sec. 22
1972	Deletes one year residency	HJR 126 am S	Aug. 22, 1972	Sept. 14, 1972	Oct. 14, 1972	Article V, sec. 1
1972	Changes representation on borough assemblies.	SJR 52	Aug. 22, 1972	Sept. 14, 1972	Oct. 14, 1972	Article X, sec. 4
1973	Provides for ratification of amendments in general	HJR 20	Aug. 27, 1974	Sept. 12, 1974	Oct. 12, 1974	Article XIII, sec. 1
1975	Permits the legislature to reconsider in special session bills vetoed by governor.	SCS CSHJR 11	Nov. 2, 1976	Nov. 23, 1976	Dec. 23, 1976	Article II, sec. 6, 9
1976	Creates Alaska Permanent Fund.	SCS CSSS HJR 39 (Resources) am S	Nov. 2, 1976	Nov. 23, 1976	Feb. 21, 1977	Article IX, sec. 7, 15

---

[9] An amendment to the Constitution becomes effective 30 days after the date of certification of the election unless otherwise provided in the amendment. (Article XIII, sec. 1)

APPENDIX B

Apportionment Schedule

In accordance with provisions of Article VI of the constitution, a reapportionment board presented a plan to the governor on June 10, 1981, for the reapportionment and redistricting of the Alaska state legislature. The report of the board includes the following description of districts and their population. *[Editor's note: at the time of publication, a lawsuit was pending against the 1981 reapportionment plan.]*

1. Ketchikan-Wrangell-Petersburg

District 1 is an area within a line proceeding from Dixon Entrance in a northerly direction up Clarence Strait, passing west of Zarembo Island, northerly up Duncan Canal, across Federick Sound to a point just north and west of Cape Fanshaw, then northeasterly to the Canadian border and southerly along the Canadian border to the point of beginning at Dixon Entrance. The district includes the Ketchikan Gateway Borough, Wrangell, Petersburg, Metlakatla, Hyder, Saxman, Meyers Chuck, and Kupreanof. It has a population of 17,940 and a variance of −2.8 percent. Candidates will run for either of two designated seats in the house and one senate seat.

2. Inside Passage-Cordova

District 2 is composed of that portion of Southeast Alaska between Dixon Entrance and Port Gravina on Prince William Sound that is not contained in Districts 1, 3, and 4. Included within its boundaries are the communities of Cordova, Yakutat, Haines, Skagway, Klukwan, Gustavus, Angoon, Kake, Thorne Bay, Klawock, Craig, and Hydaburg. The district has a population of 9,301 and a variance of +.8 percent. One house member will be elected from the district. With District 3, it will elect one senator.

3. Baranof-Chicagof

District 3 consists of Baranof Island and Chicagof Island. The communities on the islands include Sitka, Pelican, Hoonah, Tenakee Springs, and Port Alexander. The district has a population of 9,266 and variance of +.4 percent. It will elect one house member and, with District 2, one senator.

4. Juneau

District 4 boundaries coincide with those of the City and Borough of Juneau. The district has a population of 19,528 and a variance of +5.8084 percent. It will elect two house members to designated seats and one senator.

5. Kenai-Cook Inlet

District 5 includes all of the coastal areas on the east and west sides of Cook Inlet that lie south and west of Nikishka. Sterling is also within the district. The district has a population of 19,068 and a variance of +3.3 percent. Candidates will run for either of two designated seats in the house. Districts 5, 6, and 7 will elect two senators to designated seats.

6. North Kenai-South Coast

District 6 includes the northern quarter of the Kenai Peninsula, Nikishka, Hope, Cooper Landing, Moose Pass, Seward, Whittier, and Valdez. It has a population of 9,267 and a variance of +.4 percent. It will elect one house member and, with Districts 5 and 7, two senators to designated seats.

7. South Anchorage

District 7 contains the suburban southern and southeastern reaches of the Municipality of Anchorage, including the community council areas of Eldon, Old Seward/Oceanview, Rabbit Creek, Turnagain Arm, and Girdwood Valley. Its northern boundary proceeds east from the inlet on Klatt Road to the New Seward Highway, southerly on the New Seward Highway to DeArmoun Road, east on DeArmoun Road to Morgaard Road, easterly on Morgaard Road to DeArmoun Road, easterly and southerly on Rabbit Creek. The district has a population of 8,853.2 and a variance of −4.1 percent. It will elect one house member and, with Districts 5 and 6, two senators to designated seats.

8. Hillside

District 8 is bounded on the south by Rabbit Creek, Morgaard Road, and DeArmoun Road and on the west by the Seward Highway. At Tudor Road the boundary proceeds east to Bragaw Road where it turns south. This district includes the neighborhood council areas of Campbell Park, Abbott Loop, Huffman-O'Malley, Mid-Hillside, Hillside East, and Glen Alps. The district population is 18,202.1 and its variance is —1.4 percent. It will elect two house members to designated seats, and with District 9, two senators to designated seats.

9. Sand Lake

District 9 is bounded by a line beginning at the inlet and proceeding east on Klatt Road. The line proceeds north on the New Seward Highway to Dimond Boulevard where it turns west. At Minnesota Drive the line turns north and proceeds to International Airport Road where it turns west and extends to the inlet. The district includes the community council areas of Sand Lake and Klatt Road. Its population is 18,004.7 and its variance is —2.4 percent. It will elect two house members to designated seats and, with District 8, two senators to designated seats.

10. Mid-Town

District 10 is bounded by a line beginning at the intersection of the Seward Highway and Dimond Boulevard. The line proceeds west to Minnesota Drive, north to International Airport Road, east to the Alaska Railroad, north by northwest along the railroad right of way to Tudor Road, east to Arctic Boulevard, north to 36th Avenue, east on 36th Avenue to C Street, north to Northern Lights Boulevard, west to Spenard Road, north to W. 25th Street, west to Minnesota Drive, north to Chester Creek, easterly to Lake Otis Road, south to Tudor Road, west to the New Seward Highway and south to the point of beginning. The district includes the community council areas of North Star, Rogers Park, Tudor, and parts of Spenard and Taku-Campbell. It has a population of 17,685.7 and a variance of —4.1737 percent. It will elect two house members to designated seats and, with District 11, two senators to designated seats.

11. West Side

District 11 is bounded by the boundary of District 10 on the east, International Airport Road on the south, and the inlet and Chester Creek on the north. It includes the community council area of Turnagain and the major part of the Spenard area. It has a population of 17,957.8 and a variance of —2.7 percent. It will elect two house members to designated seats and, with District 10, two senators to designated seats.

12. Downtown

District 12 is bounded by Chester Creek on the south, Bragaw Road on the east, Commercial Drive and the Elmendorf reservation boundary on the north and the inlet on the west. Included are the community council areas of Government Hill, Downtown, Penland Park, and South Addition, and parts of the areas of Fairview, North Mountain View and Airport Heights. The district has a population of 18,170 and a variance of −1.5 percent. It will elect two house members to designated seats and, with District 13, two senators to designated seats.

13. Mountain View-University

District 13 is bounded by a line beginning at the intersection of Tudor Road and Lake Otis Road proceeding east to Baxter Road, north to Northern Lights Boulevard, west to Boniface Road, north to the Glenn Highway, west on the Glenn Highway, northerly and westerly around North Mountain View along the Elmendorf military reservation boundary, south to the Glenn Highway, east to Bragaw Road, south to Chester Creek, westerly to Lake Oits Road, and south to the point of beginning. The district includes the community council areas of Russian Jack Park and University, and parts of the North Mountain View and Airport Heights areas. It has a population of 18,907.5 and a variance of +2.4 percent. It will elect two house members to designated seats and, with District 12, two senators to designated seats.

14. Muldoon

District 14 includes Stuckagain Heights and the community council areas of Northeast and Scenic Park. That part of the Northeast area bounded by Boniface Road, DeBarr Road, Turpin Street, and the Glenn Highway is included in District 15. District 14 has a population of 19,031.5 and a variance of +3.1 percent. It will elect two house members to designated seats and, with District 15, two senators to designated seats.

15. Chugiak-Eagle River-Bases

District 15 includes the community council areas of Eklutna Valley, Chugiak, Birchwood, and Eagle River Valley. Also included are Fort Richardson, Elmendorf Air Force Base, and that area of the Northeast community council area bounded by Boniface Road, DeBarr Road, Turpin Street, and the Glenn Highway. The district has a population of 18,560.7 and a variance of +.56 percent. It will elect two house members to designated seats and, with District 14, two senators to designated seats.

16. Matanuska-Susitna

District 16 is comprised of the Matanuska-Susitna Borough, including the communities of Talkeetna, Willow, Houston, Big Lake, Wasilla, Bodenburg Butte, Palmer, Sutton, Peter's Creek, Montana, and Chickaloon. It has a population of 17,724.6 and a variance of —4.0 percent. It will elect two house members to designated seats and one senator.

17. Interior Highways

District 17 is made up of those areas outside of the Matanuska-Susitna Borough and the Fairbanks North Star Borough which are along the Glenn, Parks, Richardson, and Alaska Highways. Included are Paxson, Gulkana, Glennallen, Copper Center, Tonsina, Tazlina, McCarthy, Eagle, Delta, Fort Greely, Tanacross, Tok, Tetlin, Northway, Nenana, Anderson, Healy, and Cantwell. The district has a population of 9,111.9 and a variance of —1.2 percent. It will elect one house member and, with District 18, one senator.

18. Southeast North Star Borough

District 18 encompasses the southeast section of the Fairbanks North Star Borough. It includes North Pole, Eielson Air Force Base, Salcha, and Harding Lake. Its population is 9,300,with a variance of +.7 percent. It will elect one house member and, with District 17, one senator.

19. Fort Wainwright-Outer Fairbanks

District 19 includes Livengood, Ester, Goldstream Road, the Steese Highway, the eastern half of Farmers Loop Road, Fort Wainwright, Chena Hot Springs Road, Circle, Central, and Circle Hot Springs. It has a population of 8,934.3 and a variance of —3.2 percent. It will elect one house member and, with Districts 20 and 21, two senators to designated seats.

20. Fairbanks City

District 20 is bounded by the Noyes Slough and University Avenue on the west, the Fairbanks International Airport on the southwest, the Tanana River on the south, and Fort Wainwright on the east. The Creamers Field area is included as the northern edge of the district. The district has a population of 18,319.7 and a variance of —.7 percent. It will elect two house members to designated seats and, with Districts 19 and 21, two senators to designated seats.

21. West Fairbanks

District 21 includes the western half of Farmers Loop Road and the area west of Noyes Slough and University Avenue to, but not including, the Ester area. It has a population of 9,247.1 and a variance of +.2 percent. It will elect one house member and, with Districts 19 and 20, two senators to designated seats.

22. North Slope-Kotzebue

District 22 includes the areas of the North Slope Borough/Arctic Slope Regional Corporation and the Northwest Alaska Native Association. It has a population of 9,030 and a variance of −2.1 percent. The district will elect one house member and, with District 23, one senator.

23. Norton Sound

District 23 includes the area of the Bering Straits Regional Corporation; Shishmaref, Diomede, Teller, Nome, Koyuk, and Saint Michael, and the coastal communities as far south as Hooper Bay and Paimiut. Chevak is also included along with Yukon River villages down river from Mountain Village. The district has a population of 9,388 and a variance of +1.7 percent. It will elect one house member and, with District 22, one senator.

24. Interior Rivers

District 24 includes the communities on or near the great interior rivers—the Yukon, the Koyukuk, and the Kuskokwim—as far down river as Mountain Village on the Yukon and Lower Kalskag on the Kuskokwim. The Lake Clark and Lake Iliamna communities, Minto, and Manley Hot Springs are included; Eagle and Circle are not included. The district has a population of 9,549 and a variance of +3.5 percent. It will elect one house member and, with District 25, one senator.

25. Lower Kuskokwim

District 25 includes the Kuskokwim River communities down river from Tuluksak and the coastal communities from Newtok to Platinum. It has a population of 9,698 and a variance of +5.1 percent. It will elect one representative and, with District 24, one senator.

26. Bristol Bay-Aleutian Islands

District 26 includes all of the Bristol Bay Native Corporation area except Ivanof Bay, Perryville, Chignik Lake, Chignik Lagoon, and the Lake Clark-Lake Iliamna communities. Included are the remainder of the Alaska peninsula communities, the Aleutian communities, the Bristol Bay communities as far west as Twin Hills, and communities as far up river as Aleknagik and Koliganek. The Bristol Bay Borough is also included. The district has a population of 9,479 and a variance of +2.7 percent. It will elect one house member and, with District 27, one senator.

27. Kodiak-East Alaska Peninsula

District 27 covers the Kodiak Island Borough and the Alaska Peninsula communities of Ivanof Bay, Perryville, Chignik Lake, Chignik, and Chignik Lagoon. It has a population of 9,592.4 and a variance of +3.9 percent. It will elect one house member and, with District 26, one senator.

APPENDIX C

ARTICLE XV

Schedule of Transitional Measures

To provide an orderly transition from a territorial to a state form of government, it is declared and ordained:

Continuance Laws

SECTION 1. All laws in force in the Territory of Alaska on the effective date of this constitution and consistent therewith shall continue in force until they expire by their own limitation, are amended, or repealed.

Savings of Existing Rights and Liabilities

SECTION 2. Except as otherwise provided in this constitution, all rights, titles, actions, suits, contracts, and liabilities and all civil, criminal, or administrative proceedings shall continue unaffected by the change from territorial to state government, and the State shall be the legal successor to the Territory in these matters.

Local Government

SECTION 3. Cities, school districts, health districts, public utility districts, and other local subdivisions of government existing on the effective date of this constitution shall continue to exercise their powers and functions under law, pending enactment of legislation to carry out the provisions of this constitution. New local subdivisions of government shall be created only in accordance with this constitution.

Continuance of Office

SECTION 4. All Officers of the Territory, or under its law, on the effective date of this constitution shall continue to perform the duties of their offices in a manner consistent with this constitution until they are superseded by officers of the State.

Corresponding Qualifications

SECTION 5. Residence, citizenship, or other qualifications under the territory may be used toward the fulfillment of corresponding qualifications required by this constitution.

Governor to Proclaim Election

SECTION 6. When the people of the Territory ratify this constitution and it is approved by the duly constituted authority of the United States, the governor of the Territory shall, within thirty days after receipt of the official notification of such approval, issue a proclamation and take necessary measures to hold primary and general elections for all state elective offices provided for by this constitution.

First State Elections

SECTION 7. The primary election shall take place not less than forty nor more than ninety days after the proclamation by the governor of the Territory. The general election shall take place not less than ninety days after the primary election. The elections shall be governed by this constitution and by applicable territorial laws.

United States Senators and Representative

SECTION 8. The officers to be elected at the first general election shall include two senators and one representative to serve in the Congress of the United States, unless senators and a representative have been previously elected and seated. One senator shall be elected for the long term and one senator for the short term, each term to expire on the third day of January in an odd-numbered year to be determined by authority of the United States. The term of the representative shall expire on the third day of January in the odd-numbered year immediately following his assuming office. If the first represenative is elected in an even-numbered year to take office in that year, a representative shall be elected at the same time to fill the full term commencing on the third day of January of the following year, and the same person may be elected for both terms.

First Governor and Lieutenant Governor: Terms

SECTION 9. The first governor and lieutenant governor shall hold office for a term beginning with the day on which they assume office and ending at noon on the first Monday in December of the even-numbered year following the next presidential election. This term shall count as a full term for purposes of determining eligibility for reelection only if it is four years or more in duration.

(The amendment to this section was approved by the voters of the state August 25, 1970 and became effective October 10, 1970. The words "secretary of state" were changed to "lieutenant governor".)

Election of First Senators

SECTION 10. At the first state general election, one senator shall be chosen for a two-year term from each of the following senate districts, described in Section 2 of Article XIV: A, B, D, E, G, I, J, L, N, and O. At the same election, one senator shall be chosen for a four-year term from each of the following senate districts, described in Section 2 of Article XIV: A, C, E, F, H, J, K, M, N, and P.

Terms of First State Legislators

SECTION 11. The first state legislators shall hold office for a term beginning with the day on which they assume office and ending at noon on the fourth Monday in January after the next general election, except that senators elected for four-year terms shall serve an additional two years thereafter. If the first general election is held in an even-numbered year, it shall be deemed to be the general election for that year.

Election Returns

SECTION 12. The returns of the first general election shall be made, canvassed, and certified in the manner prescribed by law. The governor of the Territory shall certify the results to the President of the United States.

Assumption of Office

SECTION 13. When the President of the United States issues a proclamation announcing the results of the election, and the State has been admitted into the Union, the officers elected and qualified shall assume office.

First Session of Legislature

SECTION 14. The governor shall call a special session of the first state legislature within thirty days after the presidential proclamation unless a regular session of the legislature falls within that period. The special session shall not be limited as to duration.

First Legislators: Office Holding

SECTION 15. The provisions of Section 5 of Article II shall not prohibit any member of the first state legislature from holding any office or position created during his first term.

First Judicial Council

SECTION 16. The first members of the judicial council shall, notwithstanding Section 8 of Article IV, be appointed for terms as follows: three attorney members for one, three, and five years respectively, and three non-attorney members for two, four, and six years respectively. The six members so appointed shall, in accordance with Section 5 of Article IV, submit to the governor nominations to fill the initial vacancies on the superior court and the supreme court, including the office of chief justice. After the initial vacancies on the superior and supreme courts are filled, the chief justice shall assume his seat on the judicial council.

Transfer of Court Jurisdiction

SECTION 17. Until the courts provided for in Article IV are organized, the courts, their jurisdiction, and the judicial system shall remain as constituted on the date of admission unless otherwise provided by law. When the state courts are organized, new actions shall be commenced and filed therein, and all causes, other than those under the jurisdiction of the United States, pending in the courts existing on the date of admission, shall be transferred to the proper state court as though commenced, filed, or lodged in those courts in the first instance, except as otherwise provided by law.

Territorial Assets and Liabilities

SECTION 18. The debts and liabilities of the Territory of Alaska shall be assumed and paid by the State, and debts owed to the Territory shall be collected by the State. Assets and records of the Territory shall become the property of the State.

First Reapportionment

SECTION 19. The first reapportionment of the house of representatives shall be made immediately following the official reporting of the 1960 decennial census, or after the first regular legislative session if the session occurs thereafter, notwithstanding the provisions as to time contained in Section 3 of Article VI. All other provisions of Article VI shall apply in the first reapportionment.

State Capital

SECTION 20. The capital of the State of Alaska shall be at Juneau.

Seal

SECTION 21. The seal of the Territory, substituting the word "State" for "Territory," shall be the seal of the State.

Flag	SECTION 22. The flag of the Territory shall be the flag of the State.
Special Voting Provision	SECTION 23. Citizens who legally voted in the general election of November 4, 1924, and who meet the residence requirements for voting, shall be entitled to vote notwithstanding the provisons of Section 1 of Article V.
Ordinances	SECTION 24. Ordinance No. 1 on ratification of the constitution, Ordinance No. 2 on the Alaska-Tennessee Plan, and Ordinance No. 3 on the abolition of fish traps, adopted by the Alaska Constitutional Convention and appended to this constitution, shall be submitted to the voters and if ratified shall become effective as provided in each ordinance.
Effective Date	SECTION 25. This constitution shall take effect immediately upon the admission of Alaska into the Union as a state.

Agreed upon by the delegates in Constitutional Convention assembled at the University of Alaska, this fifth day of February, in the year of our Lord one thousand nine hundred and fifty-six, and of the Independence of the United States the one hundred and eightieth.

WM. A. EGAN
President of the Convention

R. ROLLAND ARMSTRONG
DOROTHY J. AWES
FRANK BARR
JOHN C. BOSWELL
SEABORN J. BUCKALEW, JR.
JOHN B. COGHILL
E.B. COLLINS
GEORGE D. COOPER
JOHN M. CROSS
EDWARD V. DAVIS
JAMES P. DOOGAN
TRUMAN C. EMBERG
HELEN FISCHER
VICTOR FISCHER
DOUGLAS GRAY
THOMAS C. HARRIS
JOHN S. HELLENTHAL

HERB HILSCHER
JACK HINCKEL
JAMES HURLEY
MAURICE T. JOHNSON
YULE F. KILCHER
LEONARD H. KING
WILLIAM W. KNIGHT
W.W. LAWS
ELDOR R. LEE
MAYNARD D. LONDBORG
STEVE McCUTCHEON
GEORGE M. McLAUGHLIN
ROBERT J. McNEALY
JOHN A. McNEES
M.R. MARSTON
IRWIN L. METCALF
LESLIE NERLAND

MILDRED R. HERMANN
KATHERINE D. NORDALE
FRANK PERATROVICH
CHRIS POULSEN
PETER L. READER
BURKE RILEY
RALPH J. RIVERS
VICTOR C. RIVERS
JOHN H. ROSSWOG
B.D. STEWART

JAMES NOLAN
W.O. SMITH
GEORGE SUNDBORG
DORA M. SWEENEY
WARREN A. TAYLOR
H.R. VANDERLEEST
M.J. WALSH
BARRIE M. WHITE
ADA B. WIEN

ATTEST:
THOMAS B. STEWART
Secretary of the Convention

ORDINANCE NO. 1

RATIFICATION OF CONSTITUTION

Election   SECTION 1. The Constitution for the State of Alaska agreed upon by the delegates to the Alaska Constitutional Convention on February 5, 1956, shall be submitted to the voters of Alaska for ratification or rejection at the territorial primary election to be held on April 24, 1956. The election shall be conducted according to existing laws regulating primary elections so far as applicable.

Ballot   SECTION 2. Each elector who offers to vote upon this constitution shall be given a ballot by the election judges which will be separate from the ballot on which candidates in the primary election are listed. Each of the propositions offered by the Alaska Constitutional Convention shall be set forth separately, but on the same ballot form. The first proposition shall be as follows:

"Shall the Constitution for the State of Alaska prepared and agreed upon by the Alaska Constitutional Convention be adopted?"

Yes ☐

No ☐

Canvass   SECTION 3. The returns of this election shall be made to the governor of the Territory of Alaska, and shall be canvassed in substantially the manner provided by law for territorial elections.

Acceptance and Approval

SECTION 4. If a majority of the votes cast on the proposition favor the constitution, then the constitution shall be deemed to be ratified by the people of Alaska to become effective as provided in the constitution.

Submission of Constitution

SECTION 5. Upon ratification of the constitution, the governor of the Territory shall forthwith transmit a certified copy of the constitution to the President of the United States for submission to the Congress, together with a statement of the votes cast for and against ratification.

ORDINANCE NO. 2

ALASKA-TENNESSEE PLAN

Statement of Purpose

SECTION 1. The election of senators and a representative to serve in the Congress of the United States being necessary and proper to prepare for the admission of Alaska as a state of the Union, the following sections are hereby ordained, pursuant to Chapter 46, SLA 1955:

Ballot

SECTION 2. Each elector who offers to vote upon the ratification of the constitution may, upon the same ballot, vote on a second proposition, which shall be as follows:

"Shall Ordinance Number Two (Alaska-Tennessee Plan) of the Alaska Constitutional Convention, calling for the immediate election of two United States Senators and one United States Representative, be adopted?"

Yes ☐

No ☐

Approval

SECTION 3. Upon ratification of the constitution by the people of Alaska and separate approval of this ordinance by a majority of all votes cast for and against it, the remainder of this ordinance shall become effective.

Election of Senators and Representative

SECTION 4. Two United States senators and one United States representative shall be chosen at the 1956 general election.

131

Terms	SECTION 5. One senator shall be chosen for the regular term expiring on January 3, 1963, and the other for an initial short term expiring on January 3, 1961, unless when they are seated the Senate prescribes other expiration dates. The representative shall be chosen for the regular term of two years expiring January 3, 1959.
Qualifications	SECTION 6. Candidates for senators and representative shall have the qualifications prescribed in the Constitution of the United States and shall be qualified voters of Alaska.
Other Office Holding	SECTION 7. Until the admission of Alaska as a state, the senators and representative may also hold or be nominated and elected to other offices of the United States or of the Territory of Alaska, provided that no person may receive compensation for more than one office.
Election Procedure	SECTION 8. Except as provided herein, the laws of the Territory governing elections to the office of Delegate to Congress shall, to the extent applicable, govern the election of the senators and representative. Territorial and other officals shall perform their duties with reference to this election accordingly.
Independent Candidates	SECTION 9. Persons not representing any political party may become independent candidates for the offices of senator or representative by filing applications in the manner provided in Section 38-5-10, ACLA 1949, insofar as applicable. Applications must be filed in the office of the director of finance of the Territory on or before June 30, 1956.
Party Nominations	SECTION 10. Party nominations for senators and representative shall, for this election only, be made by party conventions in the manner prescribed in Section 38-4-11, ACLA 1949, for filling a vacancy in a party nomination occurring after a primary election. The names of the candidates nominated shall be certified by the chairman and secretary of the central committee of each political party to the director of finance of the Territory on or before June 30, 1956.
Certification	SECTION 11. The director of finance shall certify the names of all candidates for senators and

representative to the clerks of court by July 15, 1956. The clerks of court shall cause the names to be printed on the official ballot for the general election. Independent candidates shall be identified as provided in Section 38-5-10, ACLA 1949. Candidates nominated at party conventions shall be identified with appropriate party designations as is provided by law for nominations at primary elections.

Ballot Form: Who Elected

SECTION 12. The ballot form shall group separately the candidates seeking the regular senate term, those seeking the short senate term, and candidates for representative. The candidate for each office receiving the largest number of votes cast for that office shall be elected.

Duties and Emoluments

SECTION 13. The duties and emoluments of the offices of senator and representative shall be as prescribed by law.

Convention Assistance

SECTION 14. The president of the Alaska Constitutional Convention, or a person designated by him, may assist in carrying out the purposes of this ordinance. The unexpended and unobligated funds appropriated to the Alaska Constitutional Convention by Chapter 46, SLA 1955, may be used to defray expenses attributable to the referendum and the election required by this ordinance.

Alternate Effective Dates

SECTION 15. If the Congress of the United States seats the senators and representative elected pursuant to this ordinance and approves the constitution before the first election of state officers, then Section 25, of Article XV shall be void and shall be replaced by the following:

> "The provisions of the constitution applicable to the first election of state officers shall take effect immediately upon the admission of Alaska into the Union as a state. The remainder of the constitution shall take effect when the elected governor takes office."

ORDINANCE NO. 3

ABOLITION OF FISH TRAPS

Ballot SECTION 1. Each elector who offers to vote upon the ratification of the constitution may, upon the same ballot, vote on a third proposition, which shall be as follows:

"Shall Ordinance Number Three of the Alaska Constitutional Convention, prohibiting the use of fish traps for the taking of solmon for commercial purposes in the coastal waters of the State, be adopted?"   Yes ☐   No ☐

Effect of Referendum SECTION 2. If the constitution shall be adopted by the electors and if a majority of all the votes cast for and against this ordinance favor its adoption, then the following shall become operative upon the effective date of the constitution:

"As a matter of immediate public necessity, to relieve economic distress among individual fishermen and those dependent upon them for a livelihood, to conserve the rapidly dwindling supply of salmon in Alaska, to insure fair competition among those engaged in commercial fishing, and to make manifest the will of the people of Alaska, the use of fish traps for the taking of salmon for commercial purposes is hereby prohibited in all the coastal waters of the State."